THE OPEN AIR

THE OPEN AIR

BY

RICHARD JEFFERIES

Introduction by
RICHARD MABEY

WILDWOOD HOUSE   LONDON

First published in Great Britain by
Chatto & Windus, 1885

Reissued in Great Britain by Wildwood House 1981

Wildwood House Ltd
1 Prince of Wales Passage
117 Hampstead Road
London NW1 3EE

ISBN 0 7045 0422 7

Introduction Copyright © 1981 by Richard Mabey

Printed and bound in Great Britain by
Biddles Ltd, Guildford, Surrey

CONTENTS

NOTE.

FOR permission to collect these papers my thanks
are due to the Editors of the following publica-
tions: *The Standard, English Illustrated Magazine,
Longman's Magazine, St. James's Gazette, Chambers's
Journal, Manchester Guardian, Good Words,* and
Pall Mall Gazette.

R. J.

INTRODUCTION TO THE WILDWOOD HOUSE EDITION

The Open Air, published in 1885, was the last selection from Richard Jefferies's non-fiction writings to appear in his lifetime. He was thirty-six at the time, and already chronically ill with the lung disease that was to kill him two years later. Perhaps he had some premonition of this, for the selection (presumably made by Jefferies himself) gives a strikingly honest and comprehensive picture of his later work. His journalistic output was prolific in the mid-'80s, and the essays included in *The Open Air* are taken from an assortment of nine different publications, from the *Times* and *Pall Mall Gazette* to the *English Illustrated Magazine*. The result is that Jefferies appears — accurately, as it happens — as something of a chameleon and a collagist. There is the jobbing writer, turning his hand, when it was asked or expected of him, to slight pieces on bathing beauties and sporting guns. There is the masterly descriptive writer in, for instance, 'Haunts of the Hare', who could construe a landscape so thoroughly in terms of the patterns of light and line that it is a wonder he did not take his sketching more seriously. There is, in rhapsodies like 'Wild Flowers', a trace of the mystic who two years previously had published *The Story of my Heart*.

Yet amidst all these familiar aspects, there is a new Jefferies, less comfortable, less certain. He had begun to see behind the pastoral facade of rural England, and could not reconcile himself to what he saw. 'The wheat is beautiful,' he writes at the end of 'One of the New Voters', 'but human life is labour.' It could not have been more starkly put; the apparent paradox of that intimate rural coexistence of toil and beauty increasingly preoccupied him, and is touched on in many of the pieces here.

If it seems a comparatively obvious insight, it is worth recalling how fast and how far Jefferies had travelled to reach it. He published his first journalism in the early '70s and his first 'country' book, *The Gamekeeper at Home*, in 1878. His rather blinkered apology for agrarian capitalism, *Hodge and his Masters*, antedates *The Open Air* by just five years. Hodge's life is nasty, short and brutishly ignorant, but that is his fault, not a consequence of a sad flaw in the world. In parts of *The Open Air*, Jefferies is not even sure about the brutishness, recognizing a culture where before he had just seen vacant faces. Earlier in 'One of the New Voters', he describes a scene in a pub after the day's work is over: 'You can smell the tobacco and see the ale; you cannot see the indefinite power which holds the men there − the magnetism of company and conversation. *Their* conversation, not *your* conversation; not the last book, the last play; not saloon conversation; but their's − talk in which neither you nor any one of your condition could really join.'

If there is a dominant theme in *The Open Air* it is this search for ways of escape, from labour, from drudgery, lifelessness and, at a more personal level, illness and social isolation. In 'Golden Brown' he writes with unashamed envy (and a new kind of blinkeredness) about the health and habits of the Kent fruit-pickers and 'the life above this life to be obtained from the constant presence with the sun-light and the stars.' It is a theme taken up again in 'Sunny Brighton': 'You do not care for nature now? Well! all I can say is, that you will have to go to nature one day — when you die. You will find nature very real then.'

Nature, to the mature Jefferies, was above all redemptive. To immerse yourself fully in it was a kind of baptism that could wash away the distortions of civilization. Humans themselves could even be an expression of nature, when not politically or economically corrupted; the 'base labourers', about whom he had once written with barely disguised contempt, appear in 'Beauty in the Country' as unblemished as figures from a Greek pastoral.

Had Jefferies lived longer, he would almost certainly have resolved the inconsistencies in his views of landscape and labour. As it is, he veers — still looking for a way of escape — between abstract aesthetics and social criticism. But there are hints of how he might have developed in those pieces where his detached, painterly skills and philosophical musings are marshalled in service of an argument, where he is prepared to stand up for a worldly delight. An open-hearted nostalgia for 'the old road, the same flowers' lifts the final paragraph of 'Wild Flowers' above mere description. And we find a more human (and more contemporary) Jefferies in

'The Modern Thames' and 'Under the Acorns' arguing for every man's right to the countryside.

But I think it is his winter pieces that come closest to our modern sympathies. Perhaps the cold and dark had a way of checking those intense flights of fancy for which he never quite found a public language. In 'Haunts of the Lapwing' the words themselves are as sharp as ice, and build up a piercingly evocative picture of the shared hardships of rain and gale. And in 'Out of Doors in February', writing of the optimism he found from the winter, he comes as close as he ever did to answering the enigma of the toiler in the field:

> 'The lark, the bird of the light, is there in the bitter short days. Put the lark then for winter, a sign of hope, a certainty of summer. Put, too, the sheathed buds there, on tree and bush, carefully wrapped around with the case that protects them as a cloak. Put, too, the sharp needles of the green corn. . . . One memory of the green corn, fresh beneath the sun and wind, will lift up the heart from the clods.'

Richard Mabey
January 1981

THE OPEN AIR.

SAINT GUIDO.

St. Guido ran out at the garden gate into a sandy lane, and down the lane till he came to a grassy bank. He caught hold of the bunches of grass and so pulled himself up. There was a footpath on the top which went straight in between fir-trees, and as he ran along they stood on each side of him like green walls. They were very near together, and even at the top the space between them was so narrow that the sky seemed to come down, and the clouds to be sailing but just over them, as if they would catch and tear in the fir-trees. The path was so little used that it had grown green, and as he ran he knocked dead branches out of his way. Just as he was getting tired of running be reached the end of the path, and came out into a wheat-field. The wheat did not grow very closely, and the spaces were filled with azure corn-flowers. St. Guido thought he was safe away now, so he stopped to look.

Those thoughts and feelings which are not sharply defined but have a haze of distance and beauty about them are always the dearest. His name was not really Guido, but those who loved him had called him so in order to try and express their hearts about him. For they thought if a great painter could be a little boy, then he would be something like this one. They were not very learned in the history of painters : they had heard of Raphael, but Raphael was too elevated, too much of the sky, and of Titian, but Titian was fond of feminine loveliness, and in the end somebody said Guido was a dreamy name, as if it belonged to one who was full of faith. Those golden curls shaking about his head as he ran and filling the air with radiance round his brow, looked like a Nimbus or circlet of glory. So they called him St. Guido, and a very, very wild saint he was.

St. Guido stopped in the cornfield, and looked all round. There were the fir-trees behind him—a thick wall of green—hedges on the right and the left, and the wheat sloped down towards an ash-copse in the hollow. No one was in the field, only the fir-trees, the green hedges, the yellow wheat, and the sun over-head. Guido kept quite still, because he expected that in a minute the magic would begin, and some-thing would speak to him. His cheeks which had been flushed with running grew less hot, but I cannot tell you the exact colour they were, for his skin was so white and clear, it would not tan under the sun, yet being always out of doors it had taken the faintest tint of golden brown mixed with rosiness. His blue eyes which had been wide open, as they always were when full of mischief, became softer, and his long eyelashes drooped over them. But as the magic did not begin, Guido walked on slowly into the wheat,

which rose nearly to his head, though it was not yet
so tall as it would be before the reapers came. He
did not break any of the stalks, or bend them down
and step on them; he passed between them, and they
yielded on either side. The wheat-ears were pale
gold, having only just left off their green, and they
surrounded him on all sides as if he were bathing.

A butterfly painted a velvety red with white spots
came floating along the surface of the corn, and
played round his cap, which was a little higher, and
was so tinted by the sun that the butterfly was
inclined to settle on it. Guido put up his hand to
catch the butterfly, forgetting his secret in his desire
to touch it. The butterfly was too quick—with a snap
of his wings disdainfully mocking the idea of catching
him, away he went. Guido nearly stepped on a
humble-bee—buzz-zz!—the bee was so alarmed he
actually crept up Guido's knickers to the knee, and
even then knocked himself against a wheat-ear when he
started to fly. Guido kept quite still while the humble-
bee was on his knee, knowing that he should not be
stung if he did not move. He knew, too, that humble-
bees have stings though people often say they have
not, and the reason people think they do not possess
them is because humble-bees are so good-natured and
never sting unless they are very much provoked.

Next he picked a corn buttercup; the flowers
were much smaller than the great buttercups which
grew in the meadows, and these were not golden
but coloured like brass. His foot caught in a
creeper, and he nearly tumbled—it was a bine of
bindweed which went twisting round and round two

stalks of wheat in a spiral, binding them together as if some one had wound string about them. There was one ear of wheat which had black specks on it, and another which had so much black that the grains seemed changed and gone leaving nothing but blackness. He touched it and it stained his hands like a dark powder, and then he saw that it was not perfectly black as charcoal is, it was a little red. Something was burning up the corn there just as if fire had been set to the ears. Guido went on and found another place where there was hardly any wheat at all, and those stalks that grew were so short they only came above his knee. The wheat-ears were thin and small, and looked as if there was nothing but chaff. But this place being open was full of flowers, such lovely azure cornflowers which the people call bluebottles.

Guido took two; they were curious flowers with knobs surrounded with little blue flowers like a lady's bonnet. They were a beautiful blue, not like any other blue, not like the violets in the garden, or the sky over the trees, or the geranium in the grass, or the bird's-eyes by the path. He loved them and held them tight in his hand, and went on, leaving the red pimpernel wide open to the dry air behind him, but the May-weed was everywhere. The May-weed had white flowers like a moon-daisy, but not so large, and leaves like moss. He could not walk without stepping on these mossy tufts, though he did not want to hurt them. So he stooped and stroked the moss-like leaves and said, "I do not want to hurt you, but you grow so thick I cannot help it." In a minute afterwards as he was walking he heard a quick rush, and saw the wheat-ears sway this way and that as if a puff of wind had struck them.

Guido stood still and his eyes opened very wide, he had forgotten to cut a stick to fight with : he watched the wheatears sway, and could see them move for some distance, and he did not know what it was. Perhaps it was a wild boar or a yellow lion, or some creature no one had ever seen ; he would not go back, but he wished he had cut a nice stick. Just then a swallow swooped down and came flying over the wheat so close that Guido almost felt the flutter of his wings, and as he passed he whispered to Guido that it was only a hare. "Then why did he run away?" said Guido; "I should not have hurt him." But the swallow had gone up high into the sky again, and did not hear him. All the time Guido was descending the slope, for little feet always go down the hill as water does, and when he looked back he found that he had left the fir-trees so far behind he was in the middle of the field. If any one had looked they could hardly have seen him, and if he had taken his cap off they could not have done so because the yellow curls would be so much the same colour as the yellow corn. He stooped to see how nicely he could hide himself, then he knelt, and in a minute sat down, so that the wheat rose up high above him.

Another humble-bee went over along the tips of the wheat—burr-rr—as he passed ; then a scarlet fly, and next a bright yellow wasp who was telling a friend flying behind him that he knew where there was such a capital piece of wood to bite up into tiny pieces and make into paper for the nest in the thatch, but his

friend wanted to go to the house because there was a
pear quite ripe there on the wall. Next came a moth,
and after the moth a golden fly, and three gnats, and
a mouse ran along the dry ground with a curious
sniffling rustle close to Guido. A shrill cry came
down out of the air, and looking up he saw two swifts
turning circles, and as they passed each other they
shrieked—their voices were so shrill they shrieked.
They were only saying that in a month their little
swifts in the slates would be able to fly. While he
sat so quiet on the ground and hidden by the wheat,
he heard a cuckoo such a long way off it sounded like
a watch when it is covered up. "Cuckoo" did not
come full and distinct—it was such a tiny little
"cuckoo" caught in the hollow of Guido's ear. The
cuckoo must have been a mile away.

Suddenly he thought something went over, and
yet he did not see it—perhaps it was the shadow
—and he looked up and saw a large bird not very
far up, not farther than he could fling, or shoot
his arrows, and the bird was fluttering his wings,
but did not move away farther, as if he had been
tied in the air. Guido knew it was a hawk, and
the hawk was staying there to see if there was a
mouse or a little bird in the wheat. After a minute
the hawk stopped fluttering and lifted his wings
together as a butterfly does when he shuts his, and
down the hawk came, straight into the corn. "Go
away!" shouted Guido jumping up, and flinging his
cap, and the hawk, dreadfully frightened and terribly
cross, checked himself and rose again with an angry
rush. So the mouse escaped, but Guido could not

find his cap for some time. Then he went on, and still the ground sloping sent him down the hill till he came close to the copse.

Some sparrows came out from the copse, and he stopped and saw one of them perch on a stalk of wheat, with one foot above the other sideways, so that he could pick at the ear and get the corn. Guido watched the sparrow clear the ear, then he moved, and the sparrows flew back to the copse, where they chattered at him for disturbing them. There was a ditch between the corn and the copse, and a streamlet; he picked up a stone and threw it in, and the splash frightened a rabbit, who slipped over the bank and into a hole. The boughs of an oak reached out across to the corn, and made so pleasant a shade that Guido, who was very hot from walking in the sun, sat down on the bank of the streamlet with his feet dangling over it, and watched the floating grass sway slowly as the water ran. Gently he leaned back till his back rested on the sloping ground—he raised one knee, and left the other foot over the verge where the tip of the tallest rushes touched it. Before he had been there a minute he remembered the secret which a fern had taught him.

First, if he wanted to know anything, or to hear a story, or what the grass was saying, or the oak-leaves singing, he must be careful not to interfere as he had done just now with the butterfly by trying to catch him. Fortunately, that butterfly was a nice butterfly, and very kindhearted, but sometimes, if you interfered with one thing, it would tell another thing, and they would all know in a moment, and stop talking, and never say a word. Once, while they were all talking pleasantly, Guido caught a fly in his hand, he felt his hand tickle as the fly stepped on it, and he shut up his little fist so quickly he caught the fly in the hollow between the palm and his fingers. The fly went buzz, and rushed to get out, but Guido laughed, so the fly buzzed again, and just told the grass, and the grass told the bushes, and everything knew in a moment, and Guido never heard another word all that day. Yet sometimes now they all knew something about him; they would go on talking. You see, they all rather petted and spoiled him. Next, if Guido did not hear them conversing, the fern said he must touch a little piece of grass and put it against his cheek, or a leaf, and kiss it, and say, "Leaf, leaf, tell them I am here."

Now, while he was lying down, and the tip of the rushes touched his foot, he remembered this, so he moved the rush with his foot and said, "Rush, rush, tell them I am here." Immediately there came a little wind, and the wheat swung to and fro, the oak-leaves rustled, the rushes bowed, and the shadows slipped forwards and back again. Then it was still, and the nearest wheat-ear to Guido nodded his head, and said in a very low tone, "Guido, dear, just this minute I do not feel very happy, although the sun-shine is so warm, because I have been thinking, for we have been in one or other of these fields of your papa's a thousand years this very year. Every year we have been sown, and weeded, and reaped, and garnered. Every year the sun has ripened us, and the rain made us grow; every year for a thousand years."

"What did you see all that time?" said Guido.

"The swallows came," said the Wheat, "and flew over us, and sang a little sweet song, and then they went up into the chimneys and built their nests."

"At my house?" said Guido.

"Oh, no, dear, the house I was then thinking of is gone, like a leaf withered and lost. But we have not forgotten any of the songs they sang us, nor have the swallows that you see to-day—one of them spoke to you just now—forgotten what we said to their ancestors. Then the blackbirds came out in us and ate the creeping creatures, so that they should not hurt us, and went up into the oaks and whistled such beautiful sweet low whistles. Not in those oaks, dear, where the blackbirds whistle to-day; even the very oaks have gone, though they were so strong that one of them defied the lightning, and lived years and years after it struck him. One of the very oldest of the old oaks in the copse, dear, is his grandchild. If you go into the copse you will find an oak which has only one branch; he is so old, he has only that branch left. He sprang up from an acorn dropped from an oak that grew from an acorn dropped from the oak the lightning struck. So that is three oak lives, Guido dear, back to the time I was thinking of just now. And that oak under whose shadow you are now lying is the fourth of them, and he is quite young, though he is so big.

"A jay sowed the acorn from which he grew up; the jay was in the oak with one branch, and some one frightened him, and as he flew he dropped the acorn which he had in his bill just there, and now you are lying in the shadow of the tree. So you see, it is a very long time ago, when the blackbirds came and whistled up in those oaks I was thinking of, and that was why I was not very happy."

"But you have heard the blackbirds whistling ever since?" said Guido; "and there was such a big black one up in our cherry tree this morning, and I shot my arrow at him and very nearly hit him. Besides, there is a blackbird whistling now—you listen. There, he's somewhere in the copse. Why can't you listen to him, and be happy now?"

"I will be happy, dear, as you are here, but still it is a long, long time, and then I think, after I am dead, and there is more wheat in my place, the blackbirds will go on whistling for another thousand years after me. For of course I did not hear them all that time ago myself, dear, but the wheat which was before me heard them and told me. They told me, too, and I know it is true, that the cuckoo came and called all day till the moon shone at night, and began again in the morning before the dew had sparkled in the sunrise. The dew dries very soon on wheat, Guido dear, because wheat is so dry; first the sunrise makes the tips of the wheat ever so faintly rosy, then it grows yellow, then as the heat increases it becomes white at noon, and golden in the afternoon, and white again under the moonlight. Besides which wide shadows come over from the clouds, and a wind always follows the shadow and waves us, and every time we sway to and fro that alters our colour. A rough wind gives us one tint, and heavy rain another, and we look different on a cloudy day to what we do on a sunny one. All these colours changed on us when the blackbird was whistling in the oak the lightning struck, the fourth one backwards from me; and it makes me sad to think that after four more oaks have gone, the same colours will come on the wheat that will grow then. It is thinking about those past colours, and songs, and leaves, and of the colours and the sunshine, and the songs, and the leaves that will come in the future that makes to-day so much. It makes to-day a thousand years long backwards, and a thousand years long forwards, and makes the sun so warm, and the air so sweet, and the butterflies so lovely, and the hum of the bees, and everything so delicious. We cannot have enough of it."

"No, that we cannot," said Guido. "Go on, you talk so nice and low. I feel sleepy and jolly. Talk away, old Wheat."

"Let me see," said the Wheat. "Once on a time while the men were knocking us out of the ear on a floor with flails, which are sticks with little hinges——"

"As if I did not know what a flail was!" said Guido. "I hit old John with the flail, and Ma gave him a shilling not to be cross."

"While they were knocking us with the hard sticks," the Wheat went on, "we heard them talking about a king who was shot with an arrow like yours in the forest—it slipped from a tree, and went into him instead of into the deer. And long before that the men came up the river—the stream in the ditch there runs into the river—in rowing ships—how you would like one to play in, Guido! For they were not like the ships now which are machines, they were rowing ships—men's ships—and came right up into the land ever so far, all along the river up to the place where the stream in the ditch runs in; just where your papa took you in the punt, and you got the waterlilies, the white ones."

"And wetted my sleeve right up my arm—oh, I know! I can row you, old Wheat; I can row as well as my papa can."

"But since the rowing ships came, the ploughs have turned up this ground a thousand times," said the Wheat; "and each time the furrows smelt sweeter, and this year they smelt sweetest of all. The horses have such glossy coats, and such fine manes, and they are so strong and beautiful. They drew the ploughs along and made the ground give up its sweetness and savour, and while they were doing it, the spiders in the copse spun their silk along from the ashpoles, and the mist in the morning weighed down their threads. It was so delicious to come out of the clods as we pushed our green leaves up and felt the rain, and the wind, and the warm sun. Then a little bird came in the copse and called, ' Sip—sip sip, sip, sip,' such a sweet low song, and the larks ran along the ground in between us, and there were blue-bells in the copse, and anemones ; till by-and-by the sun made us yellow, and the blue flowers that you have in your hand came out. I cannot tell you how many there have been of these flowers since the oak was struck by the lightning, in all the thousand years there must have been altogether—I cannot tell you how many."

"Why didn't I pick them all?" said Guido.

" Do you know," said the Wheat, " we have thought so much more, and felt so much more, since your people took us, and ploughed for us, and sowed us, and reaped us. We are not like the same wheat we used to be before your people touched us, when we grew wild, and there were huge great things in the woods and marshes which I will not tell you about lest you should be frightened. Since we have felt your hands, and you have touched us, we have felt so much more. Perhaps that was why I was not very happy till you came, for I was thinking quite as much about your people as about us, and how all the flowers of all those thousand years, and all the songs, and the sunny days were gone, and all the people were gone too, who had heard the blackbirds whistle in the oak the lightning struck. And those that are alive now— there will be cuckoos calling, and the eggs in the thrush's nests, and blackbirds whistling, and blue corn-flowers, a thousand years after every one of them is gone.

" So that is why it is so sweet this minute, and why I want you, and your people, dear, to be happy now and to have all these things, and to agree so as not to be so anxious and careworn, but to come out with us, or sit by us, and listen to the blackbirds, and hear the wind rustle us, and be happy. Oh, I wish I could make them happy, and do away with all their care and anxiety, and give you all heaps and heaps of flowers ! Don't go away, darling, do you lie still, and I will talk and sing to you, and you can pick some more flowers when you get up. There is a beautiful shadow there, and I heard the streamlet say that he would sing a little to you; he is not very big, he cannot sing very loud. By-and-by, I know, the sun will make us as dry as dry, and darker, and then the reapers will come while the spiders are spinning their silk again—this time it will come floating in the blue air, for the air seems blue if you look up.

"It is a great joy to your people, dear, when the reaping time arrives : the harvest is a great joy to you when the thistledown comes rolling along in the wind. So that I shall be happy even when the reapers cut me down, because I know it is for you, and your people, my love. The strong men will come to us gladly, and the women, and the little children will sit in the shade and gather great white trumpets of convolvulus, and come to tell their mothers how they saw the young partridges in the next field. But there is one thing we do not like, and that is, all the labour and the misery. Why cannot your people have us without so much labour, and why are so many of you unhappy ? Why cannot they be all happy with us as you are, dear ? For hundreds and hundreds of years now the wheat every year has been sorrowful for your people, and I think we get more sorrowful every year about it, because as I was telling you just now the flowers go, and the swallows go, the old, old oaks go, and that oak will go, under the shade of which you are lying, Guido ; and if your people do not gather the flowers now, and watch the swallows, and listen to the black-birds whistling, as you are listening now while I talk, then Guido, my love, they will never pick any flowers, nor hear any birds' songs. They think they will, they think that when they have toiled, and worked a

long time, almost all their lives, then they will come
to the flowers, and the birds, and be joyful in the
sunshine. But no, it will not be so, for then they will
be old themselves, and their ears dull, and their eyes
dim, so that the birds will sound a great distance off,
and the flowers will not seem bright.

"Of course, we know that the greatest part of your
people cannot help themselves, and must labour on
like the reapers till their ears are full of the dust of
age. That only makes us more sorrowful, and anxious
that things should be different. I do not suppose we
should think about them had we not been in man's
hand so long that now we have got to feel with man.
Every year makes it more pitiful because then there
are more flowers gone, and added to the vast numbers
of those gone before, and never gathered, or looked at,
though they could have given so much pleasure. And
all the work and labour, and thinking, and reading
and learning that your people do ends in nothing—
not even one flower. We cannot understand why it
should be so. There are thousands of wheat-ears in
this field, more than you would know how to write
down with your pencil, though you have learned your
tables, sir. Yet all of us thinking, and talking, cannot understand why it is when we consider how clever
your people are, and how they bring ploughs, and
steam-engines, and put up wires along the roads to
tell you things when you are miles away, and sometimes we are sown where we can hear the hum, hum,
all day of the children learning in the school. The
butterflies flutter over us, and the sun shines, and
the doves are very, very happy at their nest, but the

children go on hum, hum inside this house, and learn, learn. So we suppose you must be very clever, and yet you cannot manage this. All your work is wasted, and you labour in vain—you dare not leave it a minute.

" If you left it a minute it would all be gone; it does not mount up and make a store, so that all of you could sit by it and be happy. Directly you leave off you are hungry, and thirsty, and miserable like the beggars that tramp along the dusty road here. All the thousand years of labour since this field was first ploughed have not stored up anything for you. It would not matter about the work so much if you were only happy; the bees work every year, but they are happy; the doves build a nest every year, but they are very, very happy. We think it must be because you do not come out to us and be with us, and think more as we do. It is not because your people have not got plenty to eat and drink—you have as much as the bees. Why just look at us ! Look at the wheat that grows all over the world; all the figures that were ever written in pencil could not tell how much, it is such an immense quantity. Yet your people starve and die of hunger every now and then, and we have seen the wretched beggars tramping along the road. We have known of times when there was a great pile of us, almost a hill piled up, it was not in this country, it was in another warmer country, and yet no one dared to touch it—they died at the bottom of the hill of wheat. The earth is full of skeletons of people who have died of hunger. They are dying now this minute in your big cities, with nothing but stones all round them, stone walls and stone streets ;

not jolly stones like those you threw in the water, dear—hard, unkind stones that make them cold and let them die, while we are growing here, millions of us, in the sunshine with the butterflies floating over us. This makes us unhappy; I was very unhappy this morning till you came running over and played with us.

" It is not because there is not enough : it is because your people are so short-sighted, so jealous and selfish, and so curiously infatuated with things that are not so good as your old toys which you have flung away and forgotten. And you teach the children hum, hum, all day to care about such silly things, and to work for them and to look to them as the object of their lives. It is because you do not share us among you without price or difference ; because you do not share the great earth among you fairly, without spite and jealousy and avarice ; because you will not agree ; you silly, foolish people to let all the flowers wither for a thousand years while you keep each other at a distance, instead of agreeing and sharing them! Is there something in you—as there is poison in the nightshade, you know it, dear, your papa told you not to touch it—is there a sort of poison in your people that works them up into a hatred of one another ? Why, then, do you not agree and have all things, all the great earth can give you, just as we have the sunshine and the rain ? How happy your people could be if they would only agree ! But you go on teaching even the little children to follow the same silly objects, hum, hum, hum, all the day, and they will grow up to hate each other, and to try which can get the most round things—you have one in your pocket."

"Sixpence," said Guido. "It's quite a new one."

"And other things quite as silly," the Wheat continued. "All the time the flowers are flowering, but they will go, even the oaks will go. We think the reason you do not all have plenty, and why you do not do only just a little work, and why you die of hunger if you leave off, and why so many of you are unhappy in body and mind, and all the misery is because you have not got a spirit like the wheat, like us; you will not agree, and you will not share, and you will hate each other, and you will be so avaricious, and you will *not* touch the flowers, or go into the sunshine (you would rather half of you died among the hard stones first), and you will teach your children hum, hum, to follow in some foolish course that has caused you all this unhappiness a thousand years, and you will *not* have a spirit like us, and feel like us. Till you have a spirit like us, and feel like us, you will never, never be happy. Lie still, dear; the shadow of the oak is broad and will not move from you for a long time yet."

"But perhaps Paul will come up to my house, and Percy and Morna."

"Look up in the oak very quietly, don't move, just open your eyes and look," said the Wheat, who was very cunning. Guido looked and saw a lovely little bird climbing up a branch. It was chequered, black and white, like a very small magpie, only without such a long tail, and it had a spot of red about its neck. It was a pied woodpecker, not the large green woodpecker, but another kind. Guido saw it go round the branch, and then some way up, and round again till it came to a place that pleased it, and then the woodpecker struck the bark with its bill, tap-tap. The sound was quite loud, ever so much more noise than such a tiny bill seemed able to make. Tap-tap! If Guido had not been still so that the bird had come close he would never have found it among the leaves. Tap—tap! After it had picked out all the insects there, the woodpecker flew away over the ashpoles of the copse.

"I should just like to stroke him," said Guido. "If I climbed up into the oak perhaps he would come again, and I could catch him."

"No," said the Wheat, "he only comes once a day."

"Then tell me stories," said Guido, imperiously.

"I will if I can," said the Wheat. "Once upon a time, when the oak the lightning struck was still living, and when the wheat was green in this very field, a man came staggering out of the wood, and walked out into it. He had an iron helmet on, and he was wounded, and his blood stained the green wheat red as he walked. He tried to get to the streamlet, which was wider then, Guido dear, to drink, for he knew it was there, but he could not reach it. He fell down and died in the green wheat, dear, for he was very much hurt with a sharp spear, but more so with hunger and thirst.

"I am so sorry," said Guido; "and now I look at you, why you are all thirsty and dry, you nice old Wheat, and the ground is as dry as dry under you; I will get you something to drink."

And down he scrambled into the ditch, setting his foot firm on a root, for though he was so young, he knew how to get down to the water without wetting his feet, or falling in, and how to climb up a tree, and everything jolly. Guido dipped his hand in the streamlet, and flung the water over the wheat five or six good sprinklings till the drops hung on the wheat-cars. Then he said, "Now you are better."

"Yes, dear, thank you, my love," said the Wheat, who was very pleased, though of course the water was not enough to wet its roots. Still it was pleasant, like a very little shower. Guido lay down on his chest this time, with his elbows on the ground, propping his head up, and as he now faced the wheat, he could see in between the stalks.

"Lie still," said the Wheat, "the corncrake is not very far off, he has come up here since your papa told the mowers to mow the meadow, and very likely if you stay quiet you will see him. If you do not understand all I say, never mind, dear; the sunshine is warm, but not too warm in the shade, and we all love you, and want you to be as happy as ever you can be."

"It is jolly to be quite hidden like this," said Guido. "No one could find me; if Paul were to look all day he would never find me; even Papa could not find me. Now go on and tell me stories."

"Ever so many times, when the oak the lightning struck was young," said the Wheat, "great stags used to come out of the wood and feed on the green wheat; it was early in the morning when they came. Such great stags, and so proud, and yet so timid, the least thing made them go bound, bound, bound."

"Oh, I know!" said Guido; "I saw some jump over the fence in the forest—I am going there again soon. If I take my bow I will shoot one!"

"But there are no deer here now," said the Wheat; "they have been gone a long, long time; though I think your papa has one of their antlers."

"Now, how did you know that?" said Guido; "you have never been to our house, and you cannot see in from here because the fir copse is in the way; how do you find out these things?"

"Oh!" said the Wheat, laughing, "we have lots of ways of finding out things. Don't you remember the swallow that swooped down and told you not to be frightened at the hare? The swallow has his nest at your house, and he often flies by your windows and looks in, and he told me. The birds tell us lots of things, and all about what is over the sea."

"But that is not a story," said Guido.

"Once upon a time," said the Wheat, "when the oak the lightning struck was alive, your papa's papa's papa, ever so much farther back than that, had all the fields round here, all that you can see from Acre Hill. And do you know it happened that in time every one of them was lost or sold, and your family, Guido dear, were homeless—no house, no garden or orchard, and no dogs or guns, or anything jolly. One day the papa that was then came along the road with *his* little Guido, and they were beggars, dear, and had no place to sleep, and they slept all night in the wheat in this very field close to where the hawthorn bush grows now—where you picked the May flowers, you know, my love. They slept there all the

summer night, and the fern owls flew to and fro, and
the bats and crickets chirped, and the stars shone
faintly, as if they were made pale by the heat.   The
poor papa never had a house, but that little Guido
lived to grow up a great man, and he worked so hard,
and he was so clever, and every one loved him, which
was the best of all things.   He bought this very field
and then another, and another, and got such a lot of
the old fields back again, and the goldfinches sang
for joy, and so did the larks and the thrushes, because
they said what a kind man he was.   Then his son
got some more of them, till at last your papa bought
ever so many more.   But we often talk about the
little boy who slept in the wheat in this field, which
was his father's father's field.   If only the wheat
then could have helped him, and been kind to him,
you may be sure it would.   We love you so much
we like to see the very crumbs left by the men who
do the hoeing when they eat their crusts; we wish
they could have more to eat, but we like to see their
crumbs, which you know are made of wheat, so that
we have done them some good at least."

"That's not a story," said Guido.

"There's a gold coin here somewhere," said the
Wheat, "such a pretty one, it would make a capital
button for your jacket, dear, or for your mamma;
that is all any sort of money is good for; I wish all
the coins were made into buttons for little Guido."

"Where is it?" said Guido.

"I can't exactly tell where it is," said the Wheat.
"It was very near me once, and I thought the next
thunder's rain would wash it down into the streamlet

—it has been here ever so long, it came here first just after the oak the lightning split died. And it has been rolled about by the ploughs ever since, and no one has ever seen it; I thought it must go into the ditch at last, but when the men came to hoe one of them knocked it back, and then another kicked it along—it was covered with earth—and then, one day, a rook came and split the clod open with his bill, and pushed the pieces first one side and then the other, and the coin went one way, but I did not see; I must ask a humble-bee, or a mouse, or a mole, or some one who knows more about it. It is very thin, so that if the rook's bill had struck it, his strong bill would have made a dint in it, and there is, I think, a ship marked on it."

"Oh, I must have it! A ship! Ask a humble-bee directly; be quick!"

Bang! There was a loud report, a gun had gone off in the copse.

"That's my papa," shouted Guido. "I'm sure that was my papa's gun!" Up he jumped, and getting down the ditch, stepped across the water, and, seizing a hazel-bough to help himself, climbed up the bank. At the top he slipped through the fence by the oak and so into the copse. He was in such a hurry he did not mind the thistles or the boughs that whipped him as they sprang back, he scrambled through, meeting the vapour of the gun-powder and the smell of sulphur. In a minute he found a green path, and in the path was his papa, who had just shot a cruel crow. The crow had been eating the birds' eggs, and picking the little birds to pieces.

GOLDEN-BROWN.

Three fruit-pickers—women—were the first people I met near the village (in Kent). They were clad in "rags and jags," and the face of the eldest was in "jags" also. It was torn and scarred by time and weather; wrinkled, and in a manner twisted like the fantastic turns of a gnarled tree-trunk, hollow and decayed. Through these jags and tearings of weather, wind, and work, the nakedness of the countenance—the barren framework—was visible; the cheekbones like knuckles, the chin of brown stoneware, the upper-lip smooth, and without the short groove which should appear between lip and nostrils. Black shadows dwelt in the hollows of the cheeks and temples, and there was a blackness about the eyes. This blackness gathers in the faces of the old who have been much exposed to the sun, the fibres of the skin are scorched and half-charred, like a stick thrust in the fire and withdrawn before the flames seize it. Beside her were two young women, both in the freshness of youth and health. Their faces glowed with a golden-brown, and so great is the effect of colour that their plain features were transfigured. The sunlight under their faces made them beautiful. The summer light had been absorbed by the skin, and now shone forth from it again; as certain substances exposed to the day absorb light and emit a phosphorescent gleam in the darkness of night, so the sunlight had been drunk up by the surface of the skin, and emanated from it.

Hour after hour in the gardens and orchards they worked in the full beams of the sun, gathering fruit for the London market, resting at midday in the shade of the elms in the corner. Even then they were in the sunshine—even in the shade, for the air carries it, or its influence, as it carries the perfumes of flowers. The heated air undulates over the field in waves which are visible at a distance; near at hand they are not seen, but roll in endless ripples through the shadows of the trees, bringing with them the actinic power of the sun. Not actinic—alchemic—some intangible, mysterious power which cannot be supplied in any other form but the sun's rays. It reddens the cherry, it gilds the apple, it colours the rose, it ripens the wheat, it touches a woman's face with the golden-brown of ripe life—ripe as a plum. There is no other hue so beautiful as this human sunshine tint.

The great painters knew it—Rubens, for instance; perhaps he saw it on the faces of the women who gathered fruit or laboured at the harvest in the Low Countries centuries since. He could never have seen it in a city of these northern climes, that is certain. Nothing in nature that I know, except the human face, ever attains this colour. Nothing like it is ever seen in the sky, either at dawn or sunset; the dawn is often golden, often scarlet, or purple and gold; the sunset crimson, flaming bright, or delicately gray and scarlet; lovely colours all of them, but not like this. Nor is there any flower comparable to it, nor any gem. It is purely human, and it is only found on the human face which has felt the sunshine continually. There must, too, I suppose, be a disposition towards it, a peculiar and exceptional condition of the fibres which build up the skin; for of the numbers who work out of doors, very, very few possess it; they become brown, red, or tanned, sometimes of a parchment hue—they do not get this colour.

These two women from the fruit gardens had the golden-brown in their faces, and their plain features were transfigured. They were walking in the dusty road; there was as background a high, dusty hawthorn hedge which had lost the freshness of spring and was browned by the work of caterpillars; they were in rags and jags, their shoes had split, and their feet looked twice as wide in consequence. Their hands were black; not grimy, but absolutely black, and neither hands nor necks ever knew water, I am sure. There was not the least shape to their garments; their dresses simply hung down in straight ungraceful lines; there was no colour of ribbon or flower, to light up the dinginess. But they had the golden-brown in their faces, and they were beautiful.

The feet, as they walked, were set firm on the ground, and the body advanced with measured, deliberate, yet lazy and confident grace; shoulders thrown back —square, but not over-square (as those who have been drilled); hips swelling at the side in lines like the full bust, though longer drawn; busts well filled and shapely, despite the rags and jags and the washed-out gaudiness of the shawl. There was that in their cheeks that all the wealth of London could not purchase—a superb health in their carriage princesses could not obtain. It came, then, from the air and sunlight, and still more, from some alchemy unknown to the physician or the physiologist, some faculty exercised by the body, happily endowed with a special power of extracting the utmost richness and benefit from the rudest elements. Thrice blessed and fortunate, beautiful golden-brown in their cheeks, superb health in their gait, they walked as the immortals on earth.

As they passed they regarded me with bitter envy, jealousy, and hatred written in their eyes; they cursed me in their hearts. I verily believe—so unmistakably hostile were their glances—that had opportunity been given, in the dead of night and far from help, they would gladly have taken me unawares with some blow of stone or club, and, having rendered me senseless, would have robbed me, and considered it a righteous act. Not that there was any bloodthirstiness or exceptional evil in their nature more than in that of the thousand-and-one toilers that are met on the highway, but simply because they worked—such hard work of hands and stooping backs, and I was idle, for all they knew. Because they were going from one field of labour to another field of labour, and I walked slowly and did no visible work. My dress showed no stain, the weather had not battered it; there was no rent, no rags and jags. At an hour when they were merely changing one place of work for another place of work, to them it appeared that I had found idleness indoors wearisome and had just come forth to exchange it for another idleness. They saw no end to their labour; they had worked from childhood, and could see no possible end to labour until limbs failed or life closed. Why should they be like this? Why should I do nothing? They were as good as I was, and they hated me. Their indignant glances spoke it as plain as words, and far more distinctly than I can write it. You cannot read it with such feeling as I received their looks.

Beautiful golden-brown, superb health, what would I not give for these? To be the thrice-blessed and chosen of nature, what inestimable fortune! To be indifferent to any circumstances—to be quite thoughtless as to draughts and chills, careless of heat, indifferent to the character of dinners, able to do well on hard, dry bread, capable of sleeping in the open under a rick, or some slight structure of a hurdle, propped on a few sticks and roughly thatched with straw, and to sleep sound as an oak, and wake strong as an oak in the morning—gods, what a glorious life! I envied them; they fancied I looked askance at their rags and jags. I envied them, and considered their health and hue ideal. I envied them that unwearied step, that firm uprightness, and measured yet lazy gait, but most of all the power which they possessed, though they did not exercise it intentionally, of being always in the sunlight, the air, and abroad upon the earth. If so they chose, and without stress or strain, they could see the sunrise, they could be with him as it were—unwearied and without distress—the livelong day; they could stay on while the moon rose over the corn, and till the silent stars at silent midnight shone in the cool summer night, and on and on till the cock crew and the faint dawn appeared. The whole time in the open air, resting at mid-day under the elms with the ripple of heat flowing through the shadow; at midnight between the ripe corn and the hawthorn hedge on the white wild camomile and the poppy pale in the duskiness, with face upturned to the thoughtful heaven.

Consider the glory of it, the life above this life to be obtained from constant presence with the sunlight and the stars. I thought of them all day, and envied them (as they envied me), and in the evening I found them again. It was growing dark, and the shadow took away something of the coarseness of the group outside one of the village "pothouses." Green foliage overhung them and the men with whom they were drinking; the white pipes, the blue smoke, the flash of a match, the red sign which had so often swung to and fro in the gales now still in the summer eve, the rude seats and blocks, the reaping-hooks bound about the edge with hay, the white dogs creeping from knee to knee, some such touches gave an interest to the scene. But a quarrel had begun; the men swore, but the women did worse. It it impossible to give a hint of the language they used, especially the elder of the three whose hollow face was blackened by time and exposure. The two golden-brown girls where so heavily intoxicated they could but stagger to and fro and mouth and gesticulate, and one held a quart from which, as she moved, she spilled the ale.

WILD FLOWERS.

A FIR-TREE is not a flower, and yet it is associated in my mind with primroses. There was a narrow lane leading into a wood, where I used to go almost every day in the early months of the year, and at one corner it was overlooked by three spruce firs. The rugged lane there began to ascend the hill, and I paused a moment to look back. Immediately the high fir-trees guided the eye upwards, and from their tops to the deep azure of the March sky over, but a step from the tree to the heavens. So it has ever been to me, by day or by night, summer or winter, beneath trees the heart feels nearer to that depth of life the far sky means. The rest of spirit found only in beauty, ideal and pure, comes there because the distance seems within touch of thought. To the heaven thought can reach lifted by the strong arms of the oak, carried up by the ascent of the flame-shaped fir. Round the spruce top the blue was deepened, concentrated by the fixed point; the memory of that spot, as it were, of the sky is still fresh—I can see it distinctly—still beautiful and full of meaning. It is painted in bright colour in my mind, colour thrice laid, and indelible; as one passes

a shrine and bows the head to the Madonna, so I
recall the picture and stoop in spirit to the aspiration
it yet arouses. For there is no saint like the sky,
sunlight shining from its face.

The fir-tree flowered thus before the primroses—
the first of all to give me a bloom; beyond reach but
visible, while even the hawthorn buds hesitated to
open. Primroses were late there, a high district and
thin soil; you could read of them as found elsewhere
in January; they rarely came much before March,
and but sparingly then. On the warm red sand (red,
at least, to look at, but green by geological courtesy,
I think) of Sussex, round about Hurst of the Pierre-
points, primroses are seen soon after the year has
turned. In the lanes about that curious old mansion,
with its windows reaching from floor to roof, that
stands at the base of Wolstanbury Hill, they grow
early, and ferns linger in sheltered overhung banks.
The South Down range, like a great wall, shuts
off the sea, and has a different climate on either
hand; south by the sea—hard, harsh, flowerless,
almost grassless, bitter, and cold; on the north side,
just over the hill—warm, soft, with primroses and
fern, willows budding and birds already busy. It is
a double England there, two countries side by side.

On a summer's day Wolstanbury Hill is an island in
sunshine; you may lie on the grassy rampart, high
up in the most delicate air—Grecian air, pellucid—
alone, among the butterflies and humming bees at
the thyme, alone and isolated; endless masses of hills
on three sides, endless weald or valley on the fourth;
all warmly lit with sunshine, deep under liquid sun-

shine like the sands under the liquid sea, no harsh-
ness of man-made sound to break the insulation amid
nature, on an island in a far Pacific of sunshine.
Some people would hesitate to walk down the staircase cut in the turf to the beech-trees beneath; the
woods look so small beneath, so far down and steep,
and no handrail.   Many go to the Dyke, but none to
Wolstanbury Hill.   To come over the range reminds
one of what travellers say of coming over the Alps
into Italy; from harsh sea-slopes, made dry with salt
as they sow salt on razed cities that naught may
grow, to warm plains rich in all things, and with
great hills as pictures hung on a wall to gaze at.
Where there are beech-trees the land is always
beautiful; beech-trees at the foot of this hill, beech-
trees at Arundel in that lovely park which the Duke
of Norfolk, to his glory, leaves open to all the world,
and where the anemones flourish in unusual size and
number; beech-trees in Marlborough Forest; beech-
trees at the summit to which the lane leads that was
spoken of just now.   Beech and beautiful scenery go
together.

But the primroses by that lane did not appear till
late; they covered the banks under the thousand
thousand ash-poles; foxes slipped along there frequently, whose friends in scarlet coats could not
endure the pale flowers, for they might chink their
spurs homewards.   In one meadow near primroses
were thicker than the grass, with gorse interspersed,
and the rabbits that came out fed among flowers.
The primroses last on to the celandines and cowslips,
through the time of the bluebells, past the violets—

one dies but passes on the life to another, one sets
light to the next, till the ruddy oaks and singing
cuckoos call up the tall mowing grass to fringe
summer.

Before I had any conscious thought it was a delight
to me to find wild flowers, just to see them. It was
a pleasure to gather them and to take them home;
a pleasure to show them to others—to keep them as
long as they would live, to decorate the room with
them, to arrange them carelessly with grasses,
green sprays, tree-bloom—large branches of chestnut
snapped off, and set by a picture perhaps. Without
conscious thought of seasons and the advancing hours
to light on the white wild violet, the meadow orchis,
the blue veronica, the blue meadow cranesbill; feeling
the warmth and delight of the increasing sun-rays,
but not recognizing whence or why it was joy. All
the world is young to a boy, and thought has not
entered into it; even the old men with gray hair do
not seem old; different but not aged, the idea of age
has not been mastered. A boy has to frown and
study, and then does not grasp what long years mean.
The various hues of the petals pleased without any
knowledge of colour-contrasts, no note even of colour
except that it was bright, and the mind was made
happy without consideration of those ideals and hopes
afterwards associated with the azure sky above the
fir-tree. A fresh footpath, a fresh flower, a fresh
delight. The reeds, the grasses, the rushes—unknown
and new things at every step—something always to
find; no barren spot anywhere, or sameness. Every
day the grass painted anew, and its green seen for

the first time; not the old green, but a novel hue and
spectacle, like the first view of the sea.

If we had never before looked upon the earth, but
suddenly came to it man or woman grown, set down in
the midst of a summer mead, would it not seem to us
a radiant vision? The hues, the shapes, the song
and life of birds, above all the sunlight, the breath of
heaven, resting on it; the mind would be filled with
its glory, unable to grasp it, hardly believing that such
things could be mere matter and no more. Like a
dream of some spirit-land it would appear, scarce fit
to be touched lest it should fall to pieces, too beautiful to be long watched lest it should fade away. So it
seemed to me as a boy, sweet and new like this each
morning; and even now, after the years that have
passed, and the lines they have worn in the forehead,
the summer mead shines as bright and fresh as when
my foot first touched the grass. It has another
meaning now; the sunshine and the flowers speak
differently, for a heart that has once known sorrow
reads behind the page, and sees sadness in joy. But
the freshness is still there, the dew washes the
colours before dawn. Unconscious happiness in finding wild flowers—unconscious and unquestioning, and
therefore unbounded.

I used to stand by the mower and follow the scythe
sweeping down thousands of the broad-flowered
daisies, the knotted knapweeds, the blue scabious,
the yellow rattles, sweeping so close and true that
nothing escaped; and yet, although I had seen so
many hundreds of each, although I had lifted armfuls
day after day, still they were fresh. They never

lost their newness, and even now each time I gather
a wild flower it feels a new thing. The greenfinches
came to the fallen swathe so near to us they seemed
to have no fear; but I remember the yellowhammers
most, whose colour, like that of the wild flowers and
the sky, has never faded from my memory. The
greenfinches sank into the fallen swathe, the loose
grass gave under their weight and let them bathe in
flowers.

One yellowhammer sat on a branch of ash the livelong morning, still singing in the sun; his bright
head, his clean bright yellow, gaudy as Spain, was
drawn like a brush charged heavily with colour
across the retina, painting it deeply, for there on
the eye's memory it endures, though that was boy-
hood and this is manhood, still unchanged. The
field—Stewart's Mash—the very tree, young ash
timber, the branch projecting over the sward, I
could make a map of them. Sometimes I think
sun-painted colours are brighter to me than to
many, and more strongly affect the nerves of the
eye. Straw going by the road on a dusky winter's
day seems so pleasantly golden, the sheaves lying
aslant at the top, and these bundles of yellow tubes
thrown up against the dark ivy on the opposite wall.
Tiles, red burned, or orange coated, the sea sometimes
cleanly definite, the shadows of trees in a thin wood
where there is room for shadows to form and fall;
some such shadows are sharper than light, and have
a faint blue tint. Not only in summer but in cold
winter, and not only romantic things but plain matter-
of-fact things, as a waggon freshly painted red beside

the wright's shop, stand out as if wet with colour and delicately pencilled at the edges. It must be out of doors; nothing indoors looks like this.

Pictures are very dull and gloomy to it, and very contrasted colours like those the French use are necessary to fix the attention. Their dashes of pink and scarlet bring the faint shadow of the sun into the room. As for our painters, their works are hung behind a curtain, and we have to peer patiently through the dusk of evening to see what they mean. Out-of-door colours do not need to be gaudy—a mere dull stake of wood thrust in the ground often stands out sharper than the pink flashes of the French studio; a faggot; the outline of a leaf; low tints without reflecting power strike the eye as a bell the ear. To me they are intensely clear, and the clearer the greater the pleasure. It is often too great, for it takes me away from solid pursuits merely to receive the impression, as water is still to reflect the trees. To me it is very painful when illness blots the definition of outdoor things, so wearisome not to see them rightly, and more oppressive than actual pain. I feel as if I was struggling to wake up with dim, half-opened lids and heavy mind. This one yellowhammer still sits on the ash branch in Stewart's Mash over the sward, singing in the sun, his feathers freshly wet with colour, the same sun-song, and will sing to me so long as the heart shall beat.

The first conscious thought about wild flowers was to find out their names—the first conscious pleasure, —and then I began to see so many that I had not previously noticed. Once you wish to identify them

there is nothing escapes, down to the little white
chickweed of the path and the moss of the wall.
I put my hand on the bridge across the brook to lean
over and look down into the water. Are there any
fish? The bricks of the pier are covered with green,
like a wall-painting to the surface of the stream,
mosses along the lines of the mortar, and among the
moss little plants—what are these? In the dry sunlit lane I look up to the top of the great wall about
some domain, where the green figs look over upright
on their stalks; there are dry plants on the coping—
what are these? Some growing thus, high in the air,
on stone, and in the chinks of the tower, suspended
in dry air and sunshine; some low down under the
arch of the bridge over the brook, out of sight utterly,
unless you stoop by the brink of the water and project
yourself forward to examine under. The kingfisher
sees them as he shoots through the barrel of the
culvert. There the sun direct never shines upon
them, but the sunlight thrown up by the ripples runs
all day in bright bars along the vault of the arch,
playing on them. The stream arranges the sand in
the shallow in bars, minute fixed undulations; the
stream arranges the sunshine in successive flashes,
undulating as if the sun, drowsy in the heat, were
idly closing and unclosing his eyelids for sleep.
Plants everywhere, hiding behind every tree, under
the leaves, in the shady places, beside the dry furrows
of the field; they are only just behind something,
hidden openly. The instant you look for them they
multiply a hundredfold; if you sit on the beach and
begin to count the pebbles by you, their number

instantly increases to infinity by virtue of that conscious act.

The bird's-foot lotus was the first. The boy must have seen it, must have trodden on it in the bare woodland pastures, certainly run about on it, with wet naked feet from the bathing; but the boy was not conscious of it. This was the first, when the desire came to identify and to know, fixing upon it by means of a pale and feeble picture. In the largest pasture there were different soils and climates; it was so large it seemed a little country of itself then—the more so because the ground rose and fell, making a ridge to divide the view and enlarge by uncertainty. The high sandy soil on the ridge where the rabbits had their warren; the rocky soil of the quarry; the long grass by the elms where the rooks built, under whose nests there were vast unpalatable mushrooms—the true mushrooms with salmon gills grew nearer the warren; the slope towards the nut-tree hedge and spring. Several climates in one field: the wintry ridge over which leaves were always driving in all four seasons of the year; the level sunny plain and fallen cromlech still tall enough for a gnomon and to cast its shadow in the treeless drought; the moist, warm, grassy depression; the lotus-grown slope, warm and dry.

If you have been living in one house in the country for some time, and then go on a visit to another, though hardly half a mile distant, you will find a change in the air, the feeling, and tone of the place. It is close by, but it is not the same. To discover these minute differences, which make one locality

healthy and home happy, and the next adjoining
unhealthy, the Chinese have invented the science of
Feng-shui, spying about with cabalistic mystery, casting the horoscope of an acre. There is something
in all superstitions; they are often the foundation of
science. Superstition having made the discovery,
science composes a lecture on the reason why, and
claims the credit. Bird's-foot lotus means a fortunate spot, dry, warm—so far as soil is concerned.
If you were going to live out of doors, you might
safely build your kibitka where you found it.
Wandering with the pictured flower-book, just purchased, over the windy ridge where last year's
skeleton leaves, blown out from the alder copse
below, came on with grasshopper motion—lifted and
laid down by the wind, lifted and laid down—I sat
on the sward of the sheltered slope, and instantly
recognized the orange-red claws of the flower beside
me. That was the first; and this very morning,
I dread to consider how many years afterwards,
I found a plant on a wall which I do not know. I
shall have to trace out its genealogy and emblazon
its shield. So many years and still only at the
beginning—the beginning, too, of the beginning—for
as yet I have not thought of the garden or conserva-
tory flowers (which are wild flowers somewhere),
or of the tropics, or the prairies.

The great stone of the fallen cromlech, crouching
down afar off in the plain behind me, cast its shadow
in the sunny morn as it had done, so many summers,
for centuries—for thousands of years: worn white
by the endless sunbeams—the ceaseless flood of light

—the sunbeams of centuries, the impalpable beams polishing and grinding like rushing water: silent, yet witnessing of the Past; shadowing the Present on the dial of the field: a mere dull stone; but what is it the mind will not employ to express to itself its own thoughts?

There was a hollow near in which hundreds of skeleton leaves had settled, a stage on their journey from the alder copse, so thick as to cover the thin grass, and at the side of the hollow a wasp's nest had been torn out by a badger. On the soft and spreading sand thrown out from his burrow the print of his foot looked as large as an elephant might make. The wild animals of our fields are so small that the badger's foot seemed foreign in its size, calling up the thought of the great game of distant forests. He was a bold badger to make his burrow there in the open warren, unprotected by park walls or preserve laws, where every one might see who chose. I never saw him by daylight: that they do get about in daytime is, however, certain, for one was shot in Surrey recently by sportsmen; they say he weighed forty pounds.

In the mind all things are written in pictures— there is no alphabetical combination of letters and words; all things are pictures and symbols. The bird's-foot lotus is the picture to me of sunshine and summer, and of that summer in the heart which is known only in youth, and then not alone. No words could write that feeling: the bird's-foot lotus writes it.

When the efforts to photograph began, the difficulty

was to fix the scene thrown by the lens upon the plate.
There the view appeared perfect to the least of details,
worked out by the sun, and made as complete in
miniature as that he shone upon in nature. But
it faded like the shadows as the summer sun declines.
Have you watched them in the fields among the
flowers?—the deep strong mark of the noonday
shadow of a tree such as the pen makes drawn
heavily on the paper; gradually it loses its darkness
and becomes paler and thinner at the edge as it
lengthens and spreads, till shadow and grass mingle
together. Image after image faded from the plates,
no more to be fixed than the reflection in water of the
trees by the shore. Memory, like the sun, paints to
me bright pictures of the golden summer time of
lotus; I can see them, but how shall I fix them for
you? By no process can that be accomplished.
It is like a story that cannot be told because he who
knows it is tongue-tied and dumb. Motions of hands,
wavings and gestures, rudely convey the framework,
but the finish is not there.

To-day, and day after day, fresh pictures are
coloured instantaneously in the retina as bright and
perfect in detail and hue. This very power is often,
I think, the cause of pain to me. To see so clearly
is to value so highly and to feel too deeply. The
smallest of the pencilled branches of the bare ash-
tree drawn distinctly against the winter sky, waving
lines one within the other, yet following and partly
parallel, reproducing in the curve of the twig the
curve of the great trunk; is it not a pleasure to
trace each to its ending? The raindrops as they

slide from leaf to leaf in June, the balmy shower that
reperfumes each wild flower and green thing, drops
lit with the sun, and falling to the chorus of the
refreshed birds; is not this beautiful to see? On
the grasses tall and heavy the purplish blue pollen,
a shimmering dust, sown broadcast over the ripening
meadow from July's warm hand—the bluish pollen,
the lilac pollen of the grasses, a delicate mist of blue
floating on the surface, has always been an especial
delight to me. Finches shake it from the stalks
as they rise. No day, no hour of summer, no step
but brings new mazes—there is no word to express
design without plan, and these designs of flower and
leaf and colours of the sun cannot be reduced to set
order. The eye is for ever drawn onward and finds
no end. To see these always so sharply, wet and
fresh, is almost too much sometimes for the wearied
yet insatiate eye. I am obliged to turn away—to
shut my eyes and say I *will* not see, I will not
observe; I will concentrate my mind on my own
little path of life, and steadily gaze downwards.
In vain. Who can do so? who can care alone for
his or her petty trifles of existence, that has once
entered amongst the wild flowers? How shall I shut
out the sun? Shall I deny the constellations of the
night? They are there; the Mystery is for ever
about us—the question, the hope, the aspiration
cannot be put out. So that it is almost a pain
not to be able to cease observing and tracing the
untraceable maze of beauty.

Blue veronica was the next identified, sometimes
called germander speedwell, sometimes bird's-eye,

whose leaves are so plain and petals so blue. Many names increase the trouble of identification, and confusion is made certain by the use of various systems of classification. The flower itself I knew, its name I could not be sure of—not even from the illustration, which was incorrectly coloured; the central white spot of the flower was reddish in the plate. This incorrect colouring spoils much of the flower-picturing done; pictures of flowers and birds are rarely accurate unless hand-painted. Any one else, however, would have been quite satisfied that the identification was right. I was too desirous to be correct, too conscientious, and thus a summer went by with little progress. If you really wish to identify with certainty, and have no botanist friend and no *magnum opus* of Sowerby to refer to, it is very difficult indeed to be quite sure. There was no Sowerby, no Bentham, no botanist friend—no one even to give the common country names; for it is a curious fact that the country people of the time rarely know the names put down as the vernacular for flowers in the books.

No one there could tell me the name of the marsh-marigold which grew thickly in the water-meadows—"A sort of big buttercup," that was all they knew. Commonest of common plants is the "sauce alone"—in every hedge, on every bank, the whitish-green leaf is found—yet I could not make certain of it. If some one tells you a plant, you know it at once and never forget it, but to learn it from a book is another matter; it does not at once take root in the mind, it has to be seen several times before you are satisfied—you waver in your convictions. The leaves were

described as large and heart-shaped, and to remain
green (at the ground) through the winter; but the
colour of the flower was omitted, though it was stated
that the petals of the hedge-mustard were yellow.
The plant that seemed to me to be probably "sauce
alone" had leaves somewhat heart-shaped, but so
confusing is *partial* description that I began to think
I had hit on "ramsons" instead of "sauce alone,"
especially as ramsons was said to be a very common
plant. So it is in some counties, but, as I afterwards
found, there was not a plant of ramsons, or garlic,
throughout the whole of that district. When, some
years afterwards, I saw a white-flowered plant with
leaves like the lily of the valley, smelling of garlic, in
the woods of Somerset, I recognized it immediately.
The plants that are really common—common everywhere—are not numerous, and if you are studying
you must be careful to understand that word locally.
My "sauce alone" identification was right; to be right
and not certain is still unsatisfactory.

There shone on the banks white stars among the
grass. Petals delicately white in a whorl of rays—
light that had started radiating from a centre and
become fixed—shining among the flowerless green.
The slender stem had grown so fast it had drawn its
own root partly out of the ground, and when I tried
to gather it, flower, stem and root came away together.
The wheat was springing, the soft air full of the
growth and moisture, blackbirds whistling, wood-
pigeons nesting, young oak-leaves out; a sense of
swelling, sunny fulness in the atmosphere. The plain
road was made beautiful by the advanced boughs that

overhung and cast their shadows on the dust—boughs of ash-green, shadows that lay still, listening to the nightingale. A place of enchantment in the mornings, where was felt the power of some subtle influence working behind bough and grass and bird-song. The orange-golden dandelion in the sward was deeply laden with colour brought to it anew again and again by the ships of the flowers, the humble-bees—to their quays they come, unlading priceless essences of sweet odours brought from the East over the green seas of wheat, unlading priceless colours on the broad dandelion disks, bartering these things for honey and pollen. Slowly tacking aslant, the pollen ship hums in the south wind. The little brown wren finds her way through the great thicket of hawthorn. How does she know her path, hidden by a thousand thousand leaves? Tangled and crushed together by their own growth, a crown of thorns hangs over the thrush's nest; thorns for the mother, hope for the young. Is there a crowns of thorns over your heart? A spike has gone deep enough into mine. The stile looks farther away because boughs have pushed forward and made it smaller. The willow scarce holds the sap that tightens the bark and would burst it if it did not enlarge to the pressure.

Two things can go through the solid oak; the lightning of the clouds that rends the iron timber, the lightning of the spring—the electricity of the sunbeams forcing him to stretch forth and lengthen his arms with joy. Bathed in buttercups to the dewlap, the roan cows standing in the golden lake watched the hours with calm frontlet; watched the light

descending, the meadows filling, with knowledge of
long months of succulent clover. On their broad brows
the year falls gently; their great, beautiful eyes,
which need but a tear or a smile to make them
human,—without these, such eyes, so large and full,
seem above human life, eyes of the immortals enduring
without passion,—in these eyes, as a mirror, nature is
reflected.

I came every day to walk slowly up and down the
plain road, by the starry flowers under the ash-green
boughs; ash is the coolest, softest green. The bees
went drifting over by my head; as they cleared the
hedges they passed by my ears, the wind singing in
their shrill wings. White tent-walls of cloud—a warm
white, being full to overflowing of sunshine—stretched
across from ash-top to ash-top, a cloud-canvas roof, a
tent-palace of the delicious air. For of all things
there is none so sweet as sweet air—one great flower
it is, drawn round about, over, and enclosing, like
Aphrodite's arms; as if the dome of the sky were a
bell-flower drooping down over us, and the magical
essence of it filling all the room of the earth.
Sweetest of all things is wild-flower air. Full of their
ideal the starry flowers strained upwards on the bank,
striving to keep above the rude grasses that pushed
by them; genius has ever had such a struggle. The
plain road was made beautiful by the many thoughts
it gave. I came every morning to stay by the star-lit
bank.

A friend said, "Why do you go the same road
every day? Why not have a change and walk
somewhere else sometimes? Why keep on up and

down the same place?" I could not answer; till
then it had not occurred to me that I did always
go one way; as for the reason of it I could not tell;
I continued in my old mind while the summers went
away. Not till years afterwards was I able to see
why I went the same round and did not care for
change. I do not want change: I want the same
old and loved things, the same wild-flowers, the
same trees and soft ash-green; the turtle-doves, the
blackbirds, the coloured yellowhammer sing, sing,
singing so long as there is light to cast a shadow
on the dial, for such is the measure of his song,
and I want them in the same place. Let me find
them morning after morning, the starry-white petals
radiating, striving upwards to their ideal. Let me
see the idle shadows resting on the white dust; let
me hear the humble-bees, and stay to look down
on the rich dandelion disk. Let me see the very
thistles opening their great crowns—I should miss
the thistles; the reed-grasses hiding the moorhen;
the bryony bine, at first crudely ambitious and lifted
by force of youthful sap straight above the hedgerow
to sink of its own weight presently and progress with
crafty tendrils; swifts shot through the air with
outstretched wings like crescent-headed shaftless
arrows darted from the clouds; the chaffinch with
a feather in her bill; all the living staircase of the
spring, step by step, upwards to the great gallery
of the summer—let me watch the same succession
year by year.

Why, I knew the very dates of them all—the reddening elm, the arum, the hawthorn leaf, the

celandine, the may; the yellow iris of the waters, the heath of the hillside. The time of the nightingale —the place to hear the first note; onwards to the drooping fern and the time of the redwing—the place of *his* first note, so welcome to the sportsman as the acorn ripens and the pheasant, come to the age of manhood, feeds himself; ¯onwards to the shadowless days—the long shadowless winter, for in winter it is the shadows we miss as much as the light. They lie over the summer sward, design upon design, dark lace on green and gold; they glorify the sunlight: they repose on the distant hills like gods upon Olympus; without shadow, what even is the sun? At the foot of the great cliffs by the sea you may know this, it is dry glare; mighty ocean is dearer as the shadows of the clouds sweep over as they sweep over the green corn. Past the shadowless winter, when it is all shade, and therefore no shadow; onwards to the first coltsfoot and on to the seed-time again; I knew the dates of all of them. I did not want change; I wanted the same flowers to return on the same day, the titlark to rise soaring from the same oak to fetch down love with a song from heaven to his mate on the nest beneath. No change, no new thing; if I found a fresh wildflower in a fresh place, still it wove at once into the old garland. In vain, the very next year was different even in the same place—*that* had been a year of rain, and the flag flowers were wonderful to see; *this* was a dry year, and the flags not half the height, the gold of the flower not so deep; next year the fatal billhook came and swept away a slow-grown hedge that had given me crab-blossom in cuckoo-time and hazelnuts in harvest. Never again the same, even in the same place.

A little feather droops downwards to the ground—a swallow's feather fuller of miracle than the Pentateuch —how shall that feather be placed again in the breast where it grew? Nothing twice. Time changes the places that knew us, and if we go back in after years, still even then it is not the old spot; the gate swings differently, new thatch has been put on the old gables, the road has been widened, and the sward the driven sheep lingered on is gone. Who dares to think then? For faces fade as flowers, and there is no consolation. So now I am sure I was right in always walking the same way by the starry flowers striving upwards on a slender ancestry of stem; I would follow the plain old road to-day if I could. Let change be far from me; that irresistible change must come is bitter indeed. Give me the old road, the same flowers— they were only stitchwort—the old succession of days and garland, ever weaving into it fresh wildflowers from far and near. Fetch them from distant mountains, discover them on decaying walls, in unsuspected corners; though never seen before, still they are the same: there has been a place in the heart waiting for them.

SUNNY BRIGHTON.

SOME of the old streets opening out of the King's
Road look very pleasant on a sunny day. They run
to the north, so that the sun over the sea shines
nearly straight up them, and at the farther end,
where the houses close in on higher ground, the deep
blue sky descends to the rooftrees. The old red tiles,
the red chimneys, the green jalousies, give some
colour; and beneath there are shadowy corners and
archways. They are not too wide to whisper across,
for it is curious that to be interesting a street must
be narrow, and the pavements are but two or three
bricks broad. These pavements are not for the
advantage of foot passengers; they are merely to
prevent cart-wheels from grating against the houses.
There is nothing ancient or carved in these streets,
they are but moderately old, yet turning from the
illuminated sea it is pleasant to glance up them as
you pass, in their stillness and shadow, lying outside
the inconsiderate throng walking to and fro, and
contrasting in their irregularity with the set façades
of the front. Opposite, across the King's Road, the
mastheads of the fishing boats on the beach just rise
above the rails of the cliff, tipped with fluttering
pennants, or fish-shaped vanes changing to the wind.

They have a pulley at the end of a curved piece of
iron for hauling up the lantern to the top of the
mast when trawling; this thin curve, with a dot at
the extremity surmounting the straight and rigid
mast, suits the artist's pencil. The gold-plate shop—
there is a bust of Psyche in the doorway—often
attracts the eye in passing; gold and silver plate in
large masses is striking, and it is a very good place
to stand a minute and watch the passers-by.

It is a Piccadilly crowd by the sea—exactly the same
style of people you meet in Piccadilly, but freer in
dress, and particularly in hats. All fashionable Brighton parades the King's Road twice a day, morning
and afternoon, always on the side of the shops. The
route is up and down the King's Road as far as
Preston Street, back again and up East Street.
Riding and driving Brighton extends its Rotten Row
sometimes to Third Avenue, Hove. These well-
dressed and leading people never look at the sea.
Watching by the gold-plate shop you will not observe
a single glance in the direction of the sea, beautiful
as it is, gleaming under the sunlight. They do not
take the slightest interest in sea, or sun, or sky, or
the fresh breeze calling white horses from the deep.
Their pursuits are purely "social," and neither ladies
nor gentlemen ever go on the beach or lie where
the surge comes to the feet. The beach is ignored;
it is almost, perhaps quite vulgar; or rather it is
entirely outside the pale. No one rows, very few
sail; the sea is not "the thing" in Brighton, which
is the least nautical of seaside places. There is more
talk of horses.

The wind coming up the cliff seems to bring with it whole armfuls of sunshine, and to throw the warmth and light against you as you linger. The walls and glass reflect the light and push back the wind in puffs and eddies; the awning flutters; light and wind spring upwards from the pavement; the sky is richly blue against the parapets overhead; there are houses on one side, but on the other open space and sea, and dim clouds in the extreme distance. The atmosphere is full of light, and gives a sense of liveliness; every atom of it is in motion. How delicate are the fore legs of these thoroughbred horses passing! Small and slender, the hoof, as the limb rises, seems to hang by a thread, yet there is strength and speed in those sinews. Strength is often associated with size, with the mighty flank, the round barrel, the great shoulder. But I marvel more at the manner in which that strength is conveyed through these slender sinews; the huge brawn and breadth of flesh all depend upon these little cords. It is at these junctions that the wonder of life is most evident. The succession of well-shaped horses, overtaking and passing, crossing, meeting, their high-raised heads and action increase the impression of pleasant movement. Quick wheels, sometimes a tandem, or a painted coach, towering over the line,— so rolls the procession of busy pleasure. There is colour in hat and bonnet, feathers, flowers, and mantles, not brilliant but rapidly changing, and in that sense bright. Faces on which the sun shines and the wind blows whether cared for or not, and lit up thereby; faces seen for a moment and immediately followed by others as interesting; a flowing gallery of portraits; all life, life! Waiting unobserved under the awning, occasionally, too, I hear voices as the throng goes by on the pavement— pleasant tones of people chatting and the human sunshine of laughter. The atmosphere is full of movement, full of light, and life streams to and fro.

Yonder, over the road, a row of fishermen lean against the rails of the cliff, some with their backs to the sea, some facing it. "The cliff" is rather a misnomer, it is more like a sea-wall in height. This row of stout men in blue jerseys, or copper-hued tan frocks, seems to be always there, always waiting for the tide—or nothing. Each has his particular position; one, shorter than the rest, leans with his elbows backwards on the low rail; another hangs over and looks down at the site of the fish market; an older man stands upright, and from long habit looks steadily out to sea. They have their hands in their pockets; they appear fat and jolly, as round as the curves of their smacks drawn up on the beach beneath them. They are of such that "sleep o' nights;" no anxious ambition disturbs their placidity. No man in this world knows how to absolutely do —nothing, like a fisherman. Sometimes he turns round, sometimes he does not, that is all. The sun shines, the breeze comes up the cliff, far away a French fishing lugger is busy enough. The boats on the beach are idle, and swarms of boys are climbing over them, swinging on a rope from the bowsprit, or playing at marbles under the cliff. Bigger boys collect under the lee of a smack, and do

nothing cheerfully. The fashionable throng hastens
to and fro, but the row leaning against the railings
do not stir.

Doleful tales they have to tell any one who inquires
about the fishing. There have been " no herrings "
these two years. One man went out with his smack,
and after working for hours returned with *one sole.*
I can never get this one sole out of my mind when
I see the row by the rails. While the fisherman was
telling me this woeful story, I fancied I heard voices
from a crowd of the bigger boys collected under a
smack, voices that said, "Ho! ho! Go on! you're
kidding the man!" Is there much "kidding" in this
business of fish? Another man told me (but he was
not a smack proprietor) that £50, £70, or £80 was a
common night's catch. Some people say that the
smacks never put to sea until the men have spent
every shilling they have got, and are obliged to sail.
If truth lies at the bottom of a well, it is the well of
a fishing boat, for there is nothing so hard to get at
as the truth about fish. At the time when society
was pluming itself on the capital results attained by
the Fisheries Exhibition in London, and gentlemen
described in the papers how they had been to market
and purchased cod at sixpence a pound, one shilling
and eightpence a pound was the price in the Brighton
fishmongers' shops, close to the sea. Not the least
effect was produced in Brighton; fish remains at
precisely the same price as before all this ridiculous
trumpeting. But while the fishmongers charge two-
pence each for fresh herrings, the old women bring
them to the door at sixteen a shilling. The poor who

live in the old part of Brighton, near the markets, use great quantities of the smaller and cheaper fish, and their children weary of the taste to such a degree that when the girls go out to service they ask to be excused from eating it.

The fishermen say they can often find a better market by sending their fish to Paris; much of the fish caught off Brighton goes there. It is fifty miles to London, and 250 to Paris; how then can this be? Fish somehow slip through ordinary rules, being slimy of surface; the maxims of the writers on demand and supply are quite ignored, and there is no groping to the bottom of this well of truth.

Just at the corner of some of the old streets that come down to the King's Road one or two old fishermen often stand. The front one props himself against the very edge of the buildings, and peers round into the broad sunlit thoroughfare; his brown copper frock makes a distinct patch of colour at the edge of the house. There is nothing in common between him and the moving throng: he is quite separate and belongs to another race; he has come down from the shadow of the old street, and his copper-hued frock might have come out of the last century.

The fishing-boats and the fishing, the nets, and all the fishing work are a great ornament to Brighton. They are real; there is something about them that forms a link with the facts of the sea, with the forces of the tides and winds, and the sunlight gleaming on the white crests of the waves. They speak to thoughts lurking in the mind; they float between life and death as with a billow on either hand; their anchors go down to the roots of existence. This is real work, real labour of man, to draw forth food from the deep as the plough draws it from the earth. It is in utter contrast to the artificial work—the feathers, the jewellery, the writing at desks of the town. The writings of a thousand clerks, the busy factory work, the trimmings and feathers, and counter-attendance do not touch the real. They are all artificial. For food you must still go to the earth and to the sea, as in primeval days. Where would your thousand clerks, your trimmers, and counter-salesmen be without a loaf of bread, without meat, without fish? The old brown sails and the nets, the anchors and tarry ropes, go straight to nature. You do not care for nature now? Well! all I can say is, you will have to go to nature one day—when you die: you will find nature very real then. I rede you to recognize the sunlight and the sea, the flowers and woods *now*.

I like to go down on the beach among the fishing boats, and to recline on the shingle by a smack when the wind comes gently from the west, and the low wave breaks but a few yards from my feet. I like the occasional passing scent of pitch: they are melting it close by. I confess I like tar: one's hands smell nice after touching ropes. It is more like home down on the beach here; the men are doing something real, sometimes there is the clink of a hammer; behind me there is a screen of brown net, in which rents are being repaired; a big rope yonder stretches as the horse goes round, and the heavy smack is drawn slowly up over the pebbles. The full curves of the rounded bows beside me are pleasant to the eye, as any curve is that recalls those of woman. Mastheads stand up against the sky, and a loose rope swings as the breeze strikes it; a veer of the wind brings a puff of smoke from the funnel of a cabin, where some one is cooking, but it is not disagreeable, like smoke from a house chimney-pot; another veer carries it away again,—depend upon it the simplest thing cooked there is nice. Shingle rattles as it is shovelled up for ballast —the sound of labour makes me more comfortably lazy. They are not in a hurry, nor "chivy" over their work either; the tides rise and fall slowly, and they work in correspondence. No infernal fidget and fuss. Wonder how long it would take me to pitch a pebble so as to lodge on the top of that large brown pebble there? I try, once now and then.

Far out over the sea there is a peculiar bank of clouds. I was always fond of watching clouds; these do not move much. In my pocket-book I see I have several notes about these peculiar sea-clouds. They form a band not far above the horizon, not very thick but elongated laterally. The upper edge is curled or wavy, not so heavily as what is called mountainous, not in the least threatening; this edge is white. The body of the vapour is a little darker, either because thicker, or because the light is reflected at a different angle. But it is the lower edge which is singular: in direct contrast with the curled or wavy edge above, the under edge is perfectly straight and parallel to the line of the horizon. It looks as if the level of the sea

made this under line.   This bank moves very slowly—
scarcely perceptibly—but in course of hours rises, and
as it rises spreads, when the extremities break off in
detached pieces, and these gradually vanish.   Sometimes when travelling I have pointed out the direction
of the sea, feeling sure it was there, and not far off,
though invisible, on account of the appearance of the
clouds, whose under edge was cut across so straight.
When this peculiar bank appears at Brighton it is an
almost certain sign of continued fine weather, and I
have noticed the same thing elsewhere; once particularly it remained fine after this appearance despite
every threat the sky could offer of a storm.   All the
threats came to nothing for three weeks, not even
thunder and lightning could break it up,—"deceitful
flashes," as the Arabs say; for, like the sons of the
desert, just then the farmers longed for rain on their
parched fields.   To me, while on the beach among the
boats, the value of these clouds lies in their slow-
ness of movement, and consequent effect in soothing the mind.   Outside the hurry and drive of life
a rest comes through the calm of nature.   As the
swell of the sea carries up the pebbles, and arranges
the largest farthest inland, where they accumulate
and stay unmoved, so the drifting of the clouds, and
the touch of the wind, the sound of the surge, arrange
the molecules of the mind in still layers.   It is then
that a dream fills it, and a dream is sometimes better
than the best reality.   Laugh at the idea of dreaming
where there is an odour of tar if you like, but you see
it is outside intolerable civilization.   It is a hundred
miles from the King's Road, though but just under it.

There is a scheme on foot for planking over the ocean, beginning at the bottom of West Street. An immense central pier is proposed, which would occupy the only available site for beaching the smacks. If carried out, the whole fishing industry must leave Brighton,—to the fishermen the injury would be beyond compensation, and the aspect of Brighton itself would be destroyed. Brighton ought to rise in revolt against it.

All Brighton chimney-pots are put on with giant cement, in order to bear the strain of the tremendous winds rushing up from the sea. Heavy as the gales are, they seldom do much mischief to the roofs, such as are recorded inland. On the King's Road a plate-glass window is now and then blown in, so that on hurricane days the shutters are generally half shut. It is said that the wind gets between the iron shutters and the plate glass and shakes the windows loose. The heaviest waves roll in by the West Pier, and at the bottom of East Street. Both sides of the West Pier are washed by larger waves than can be seen all along the coast from the Quarter Deck. Great rollers come in at the concrete groyne at the foot of East Street. Exposed as the coast is, the waves do not convey so intense an idea of wildness, confusion, and power as they do at Dover. To see waves in their full vigour go to the Admiralty Pier and watch the seas broken by the granite wall. Windy Brighton has not an inch of shelter anywhere in a gale, and the salt rain driven by the wind penetrates the thickest coat. The windiest spot is at the corner of Second Avenue, Hove; the wind just there is almost enough to choke

those who face it. Double windows—Russian fashion
—are common all along the sea-front, and are needed.

After a gale, when the wind changes, as it usually
does, it is pleasant to see the ships work in to the
verge of the shore. The sea is turbid and yellow with
sand beaten up by the recent billows,—this yellow-
ness extends outwards to a certain line, and is there
succeeded by the green of clearer water. Beyond this
again the surface looks dark, as if still half angry, and
clouds hang over it, loth to retire from the strife. As
bees come out of their hives when the rain ceases and
the sun shines, so the vessels which have been lying-to
in harbour, or under shelter of promontories, are now
eagerly making their way down Channel, and, in order
to get as long a tack and as much advantage as
possible, they are brought to the edge of the shallow
water. Sometimes fifteen or twenty or more stand
in; all sizes from the ketch to the three-master. The
wind is not strong, but that peculiar drawing breeze
which seems to pull a ship along as if with a tow-
rope. The brig stands straight for the beach, with
all sail set; she heels a little, not much; she scarcely
heaves to the swell, and is not checked by meeting
waves; she comes almost to the yellow line of turbid
water, when round she goes, and you can see the sails
shiver as the breeze touches them on both surfaces
for a moment. Then again she shows her stern and
away she glides, while another approaches: and all day
long they pass. There is always something shadowy,
not exactly unreal, but shadowy about a ship; it
seems to carry a romance, and the imagination
fashions a story to the swelling sails.

The bright light of Brighton brings all things into clear relief, giving them an edge and outline; as steel burns with a flame like wood in oxygen, so the minute particles of iron in the atmosphere seem to burn and glow in the sunbeams, and a twofold illumination fills the air. Coming back to the place after a journey this brilliant light is very striking, and most new visitors notice it. Even a room with a northern aspect is full of light, too strong for some eyes, till accustomed to it. I am a great believer in light—sunlight—and of my free will never let it be shut out with curtains. Light is essential to life, like air; life is thought; light is as fresh air to the mind. Brilliant sunshine is reflected from the houses and fills the streets. The walls of the houses are clean and less discoloured by the deposit of carbon than usual in most towns, so that the reflection is stronger from these white surfaces. Shadow there is none in summer, for the shadows are lit up by diffusion. Something in the atmosphere throws light down into shaded places as if from a mirror. Waves beat ceaselessly on the beach, and the undulations of light flow continuously forwards into the remotest corners. Pure air, free from suspended matter, lets the light pass freely, and perhaps this absence of suspended material is the reason that the heat is not so oppressive as would be supposed considering the glare. Certainly it is not so hot as London; on going up to town on a July or August day it seems much hotter there, so much so that one pants for air. Conversely in winter, London appears much colder, the thick dark atmosphere seems to increase the bitterness of the easterly winds, and returning to Brighton is entering a warmer because clearer air. Many complain of the brilliance of the light; they say the glare is overpowering, but the eyes soon become acclimatized. This glare is one of the great recommendations of Brighton; the strong light is evidently one of the causes of its healthfulness to those who need change. There is no such glowing light elsewhere along the south coast; these things are very local.

A demand has been made for trees, to plant the streets and turn them into boulevards for shade, than which nothing could be more foolish. It is the dryness of the place that gives it its character. After a storm, after heavy rain for days, in an hour the pavements are not only dry but clean; no dirt, sticky and greasy, remains. The only dirt in Brighton, for three-fourths of the year, is that made by the water-carts. Too much water is used, and a good clean road covered with mud an inch thick in August; but this is not the fault of Brighton—it is the lack of observation on the part of the Cadi who ought to have noticed the wretched condition of ladies' boots when compelled to cross these miry promenades. Trees are not wanted in Brighton; it is the peculiar glory of Brighton to be treeless. Trees are the cause of damp, they suck down moisture, and fill a circle round them with humidity. Places full of trees are very trying in spring and autumn even to robust people, much more so to convalescents and delicate persons. Have nothing to do with trees, if Brighton is to retain its value. Glowing light, dry, clear, and clean air, general dryness—these are the qualities that rendered

Brighton a sanatorium; light and glow without oppressive, moist heat; in winter a clear cold. Most terrible of all to bear is cold when the atmosphere is saturated with water. If any reply that trees have no leaves in winter and so do not condense moisture, I at once deny the conclusion; they have no leaves, but they condense moisture nevertheless. This is effected by the minute twigs, thousands of twigs and little branches, on which the mists condense, and distil in drops. Under a large tree, in winter, there is often a perfect shower, enough to require an umbrella, and it lasts for hours. Eastbourne is a pleasant place, but visit Eastbourne, which is proud of its trees, in October, and feel the damp fallen leaves under your feet, and you would prefer no trees.

Let nothing check the descent of those glorious beams of sunlight which fall at Brighton. Watch the pebbles on the beach; the foam runs up and wets them, almost before it can slip back the sunshine has dried them again. So they are alternately wetted and dried. Bitter sea and glowing light, bright clear air, dry as dry,—that describes the place. Spain is the country of sunlight, burning sunlight; Brighton is a Spanish town in England, a Seville. Very bright colours can be worn in summer because of this powerful light; the brightest are scarcely noticed, for they seem to be in concert with the sunshine. Is it difficult to paint in so strong a light? Pictures in summer look dull and out of tune when this Seville sun is shining. Artificial colours of the palette cannot live in it. As a race we do not seem to care much for colour or art—I mean in the common things of daily life—else a great deal of colour might be effectively used in Brighton in decorating houses and woodwork. Much more colour might be put in the windows, brighter flowers and curtains; more, too, inside the rooms; the sober hues of London furniture and carpets are not in accord with Brighton light. Gold and ruby and blue, the blue of transparent glass, or purple, might be introduced, and the romance of colour freely indulged. At high tide of summer Spanish mantillas, Spanish fans, would not be out of place in the open air. No tint is too bright—scarlet, cardinal, anything the imagination fancies; the brightest parasol is a matter of course. Stand, for instance, by the West Pier, on the Esplanade, looking east on a full-lit August day. The sea is blue, streaked with green, and is stilled with heat; the low undulations can scarcely rise and fall for somnolence. The distant cliffs are white; the houses yellowish-white; the sky blue, more blue than fabled Italy. Light pours down, and the bitter salt sea wets the pebbles; to look at them makes the mouth dry, in the unconscious recollection of the saltness and bitterness. The flags droop, the sails of the fishing-boats hang idle; the land and the sea are conquered by the great light of the sun.

Some people become famous by being always in one attitude. Meet them when you will, they have invariably got an arm—the same arm—crossed over the breast, and the hand thrust in between the buttons of the coat to support it. Morning, noon, or evening, in the street, the carriage, sitting, reading the paper, always the same attitude; thus they achieve social distinction; it takes the place of a medal or the red ribbon. What is a general or a famous orator compared to a man always in the same attitude? Simply nobody, nobody knows him, everybody knows the mono-attitude man. Some people make their mark by invariably wearing the same short pilot coat. Doubtless it has been many times renewed, still it is the same coat. In winter it is thick, in summer thin, but identical in cut and colour. Some people sit at the same window of the reading-room at the same hour every day, all the year round. This is the way to become marked and famous; winning a battle is nothing to it. When it was arranged that a military band should play on the Brunswick Lawns, it became the fashion to stop carriages in the road and listen to it. Frequently there were carriages four deep, while the gale blew the music out to sea and no one heard a note. Still they sat content.

There are more handsome women in Brighton than anywhere else in the world. They are so common that gradually the standard of taste in the mind rises, and good-looking women who would be admired in other places pass by without notice. Where all the flowers are roses, you do not see a rose. They are all plump, not to say fat, which would be rude; very plump, and have the glow and bloom of youth upon the cheeks. They do not suffer from "pernicious anæmia," that evil bloodlessness which London physicians are not unfrequently called upon to cure, when the cheeks are white as paper and have to be rosied with minute doses of arsenic. They extract their arsenic from the air. The way they step and the carriage of the form show how full they are of life and spirits. Sarah Bernhardt will not come to Brighton if she can help it, lest she should lose that high art angularity and slipperiness of shape which suits her *rôle*. Dresses seem always to fit well, because people somehow expand to them. It is pleasant to see the girls walk, because the limbs do not drag, the feet are lifted gaily and with ease. Horse-exercise adds a deeper glow to the face; they ride up on the Downs first, out of pure cunning, for the air there is certain to impart a freshness to the features like dew on a flower, and then return and walk their horses to and fro the King's Road, certain of admiration. However often these tricks are played, they are always successful. Those philanthropic folk who want to reform women's dress, and call upon the world to observe how the present style contracts the chest, and forces the organs of the body out of place (what a queer expression it seems, " organs " !) have not a chance in Brighton. Girls lace tight and " go in " for the tip of the fashion, yet they bloom and flourish as green bay trees, and do not find their skirts any obstacle in walking or tennis. The horse-riding that goes on is a thing to be chronicled; they are always on horseback, and you may depend upon it that it is better for them than all the gymnastic exercises ever invented. The liability to strain, and even serious internal injury, which is incurred in gymnastic exercises, ought to induce sensible people to be extremely careful how they permit their daughters to sacrifice themselves on this scientific altar. Buy them horses to ride, if you want them to enjoy good health and sound constitutions. Nothing like horses for women. Send the professors to Suakim, and put the girls on horseback. Whether Brighton grows handsome girls, or whether they flock there drawn by instinct, or become lovely by staying there, is an inquiry too difficult to pursue.

There they are, one at least in every group, and you have to walk, as the Spaniards say, with your beard over your shoulder, continually looking back at those who have passed. The only antidote known is to get married before you visit the place, and doubts have been expressed as to its efficacy. In the south-coast Seville there is nothing done but heart-breaking; it is so common it is like hammering flints for road-mending; nobody cares if your heart is in pieces. They break hearts on horseback, and while walking, playing tennis, shopping—actually at shopping, not to mention parties of every kind. No one knows where the next danger will be encountered—at the very next corner perhaps. Feminine garments have an irresistible flutter in the sea-breeze ; feathers have a beckoning motion. No one can be altogether good in Brighton, and that is the great charm of it. The language of the eyes is cultivated to a marvellous degree ; as we say of dogs, they quite talk with their eyes. Even when you do not chance to meet an exceptional beauty, still the plainer women are not plain like the plain women in other places. The average is higher among them, and they are not so irredeemably uninteresting. The flash of an eye, the shape of a shoulder, the colour of the hair—something or other pleases. Women without a single good feature are often good-looking in New Seville because of an indescribable style or manner. They catch the charm of the good-looking by living among them, so that if any young lady desires to acquire the art of attraction she has only to take train and join them. Delighted with our protectorate of Paphos, Venus has lately decided to reside on these shores. Every morning the girls' schools go for their constitutional walks; there seem no end of these schools—the place has a garrison of girls, and the same thing is noticeable in their ranks. Too young to have developed actual loveliness, some in each band distinctly promise future success. After long residence the people become accustomed to good looks, and do not see anything especial around them, but on going away for a few days soon miss these pleasant faces.

In reconstructing Brighton station, one thing was omitted—a balcony from which to view the arrival and departure of the trains in summer and autumn. The scene is as lively and interesting as the stage when a good play is proceeding. So many happy expectant faces, often very beautiful; such a mingling of colours, and succession of different figures; now a brunette, now golden hair: it is a stage, only it is real. The bustle, which is not the careworn anxious haste of business; the rushing to and fro; the greetings of friends; the smiles; the shifting of the groups, some coming, and some going—plump and rosy,—it is really charming. One has a fancy dog, another a bright-bound novel; very many have cavaliers; and look at the piles of luggage!

What dresses, what changes and elegance concealed therein !—conjurors' trunks out of which wonders will spring. Can anything look jollier than a cab overgrown with luggage, like huge barnacles, just starting away with its freight? One can imagine such a fund of enjoyment on its way in that cab. This happy throng seems to express something that delights the heart. I often used to walk up to the station just to see it, and left feeling better.

THE PINE WOOD.

THERE was a humming in the tops of the young pines
as if a swarm of bees were busy at the green cones.
They were not visible through the thick needles, and
on listening longer it seemed as if the sound was not
exactly the note of the bee—a slightly different pitch,
and the hum was different, while bees have a habit
of working close together. Where there is one bee
there are usually five or six, and the hum is that of
a group; here there only appeared one or two insects
to a pine. Nor was the buzz like that of the humble-
bee, for every now and then one came along low down,
flying between the stems, and his note was much
deeper. By-and-by, crossing to the edge of the
plantation, where the boughs could be examined,
being within reach, I found it was wasps. A yellow
wasp wandered over the blue-green needles till he
found a pair with a drop of liquid like dew between
them. There he fastened himself and sucked at it;
you could see the drop gradually drying up till it
was gone. The largest of these drops were generally
between two needles—those of the Scotch fir or pine
grow in pairs—but there were smaller drops on the
outside of other needles. In searching for this exuding

turpentine the wasps filled the whole plantation with
the sound of their wings. There must have been
many thousands of them. They caused no inconve-
nience to any one walking in the copse, because they
were high overhead.

Watching these wasps I found two cocoons of pale
yellow silk on a branch of larch, and by them a green
spider. He was quite green—two shades, lightest on
the back, but little lighter than the green larch bough.
An ant had climbed up a pine and over to the extreme
end of a bough; she seemed slow and stupefied in her
motions, as if she had drunken of the turpentine and
had lost her intelligence. The soft cones of the larch
could be easily cut down the centre with a penknife,
showing the structure of the cone and the seeds inside
each scale. It is for these seeds that birds frequent
the fir copses, shearing off the scales with their beaks.
One larch cone had still the tuft at the top—a pine-
apple in miniature. The loudest sound in the wood
was the humming in the trees; there was no wind,
no sunshine; a summer day, still and shadowy, under
large clouds high up. To this low humming the
sense of hearing soon became accustomed, and it
served but to render the silence deeper. In time, as
I sat waiting and listening, there came the faintest
far-off song of a bird away in the trees; the merest
thin upstroke of sound, slight in structure, the echo
of the strong spring singing. This was the summer
repetition, dying away. A willow-wren still remembered his love, and whispered about it to the silent
fir tops, as in after days we turn over the pages of
letters, withered as leaves, and sigh. So gentle, so

low, so tender a song the willow-wren sang that it could scarce be known as the voice of a bird, but was like that of some yet more delicate creature with the heart of a woman.

A butterfly with folded wings clung to a stalk of grass; upon the under side of his wing thus exposed there were buff spots, and dark dots and streaks drawn on the finest ground of pearl-grey, through which there came a tint of blue; there was a blue, too, shut up between the wings, visible at the edges. The spots, and dots, and streaks were not exactly the same on each wing; at first sight they appeared similar, but, on comparing one with the other, differences could be traced. The pattern was not mechanical; it was hand-painted by Nature, and the painter's eye and fingers varied in their work.

How fond Nature is of spot-markings!—the wings of butterflies, the feathers of birds, the surface of eggs, the leaves and petals of plants are constantly spotted; so, too, fish—as trout. From the wing of the butterfly I looked involuntarily at the foxglove I had just gathered; inside, the bells were thickly spotted—dots and dustings that might have been transferred to a butterfly's wing. The spotted meadow-orchis; the brown dots on the cowslips; brown, black, greenish, reddish dots and spots and dustings on the eggs of the finches, the whitethroats, and so many others—some of the spots seem as if they had been splashed on and had run into short streaks, some mottled, some gathered together at the end; all spots, dots, dustings of minute specks, mottlings, and irregular markings. The histories, the stories, the library of knowledge

contained in those signs! It was thought a wonderful
thing when at last the strange inscriptions of Assyria
were read, made of nail-headed characters whose sound
was lost; it was thought a triumph when the yet older
hieroglyphics of Egypt were compelled to give up their
messages, and the world hoped that we should know
the secrets of life. That hope was disappointed; there
was nothing in the records but superstition and useless
ritual. But here we go back to the beginning; the
antiquity of Egypt is nothing to the age of these
signs—they date from unfathomable time. In them
the sun has written his commands, and the wind
inscribed deep thought. They were before superstition
began; they were composed in the old, old world,
when the Immortals walked on earth. They have
been handed down thousands upon thousands of years
to tell us that to-day we are still in the presence of
the heavenly visitants, if only we will give up the
soul to these pure influences. The language in which
they are written has no alphabet, and cannot be
reduced to order. It can only be understood by the
heart and spirit. Look down into this foxglove bell
and you will know that; look long and lovingly at
this blue butterfly's underwing, and a feeling will
rise to your consciousness.

Some time passed, but the butterfly did not move;
a touch presently disturbed him, and flutter, flutter
went his blue wings, only for a few seconds, to another
grass-stalk, and so on from grass-stalk to grass-stalk
as compelled, a yard flight at most. He would not
go farther; he settled as if it had been night. There
was no sunshine, and under the clouds he had no

animation. A swallow went by singing in the air, and
as he flew his forked tail was shut, and but one streak
of feathers drawn past. Though but young trees, there
was a coating of fallen needles under the firs an inch
thick, and beneath it the dry earth touched warm. A
fern here and there came up through it, the palest of
pale green, quite a different colour to the same species
growing in the hedges away from the copse. A yellow
fungus, streaked with scarlet as if blood had soaked
into it, stood at the foot of a tree occasionally. Black
fungi, dry, shrivelled, and dead, lay fallen about,
detached from the places where they had grown, and
crumbling if handled. Still more silent after sunset,
the wood was utterly quiet; the swallows no longer
passed twittering, the willow-wren was gone, there was
no hum or rustle; the wood was as silent as a shadow.

But before the darkness a song and an answer
arose in a tree, one bird singing a few notes and
another replying side by side. Two goldfinches sat
on the cross of a larch-fir and sang, looking towards
the west, where the light lingered. High up, the
larch-fir boughs with the top shoot form a cross; on
this one goldfinch sat, the other was immediately
beneath. At even the birds often turn to the west
as they sing.

Next morning the August sun shone, and the wood
was all a-hum with insects. The wasps were working
at the pine boughs high overhead; the bees by dozens
were crowding to the bramble flowers; swarming on
them, they seemed so delighted; humble-bees went
wandering among the ferns in the copse and in the
ditches—they sometimes alight on fern—and calling

at every purple heath-blossom, at the purple knapweeds, purple thistles, and broad handfuls of yellow-
weed flowers. Wasp-like flies barred with yellow
suspended themselves in the air between the pine-
trunks like hawks hovering, and suddenly shot
themselves a yard forward or to one side, as if the
rapid vibration of their wings while hovering had
accumulated force which drove them as if discharged
from a cross-bow. The sun had set all things in
motion.

There was a hum under the oak by the hedge,
a hum in the pine wood, a humming among the heath
and the dry grass which heat had browned. The air
was alive and merry with sound, so that the day
seemed quite different and twice as pleasant. Three
blue butterflies fluttered in one flowery corner, the
warmth gave them vigour ; two had a silvery edging
to their wings, one was brown and blue. The nuts
reddening at the tips appeared ripening like apples
in the sunshine. This corner is a favourite with wild
bees and butterflies ; if the sun shines they are sure
to be found there at the heath-bloom and tall yellow-
weed, and among the dry seeding bennets or grass-
stalks. All things, even butterflies, are local in their
habits. Far up on the hillside the blue green of the
pines beneath shone in the sun—a burnished colour ;
the high hillside is covered with heath and heather.
Where there are open places a small species of gorse,
scarcely six inches high, is in bloom, the yellow
blossom on the extremity of the stalk.

Some of these gorse plants seemed to have a different
flower growing at the side of the stem, instead of at

the extremity. These florets were cream-coloured, so that it looked like a new species of gorse. On gathering it to examine the thick-set florets, it was found that a slender runner or creeper had been torn up with it. Like a thread the creeper had wound itself round and round the furze, buried in and hidden by the prickles, and it was this creeper that bore the white or cream-florets. It was tied round as tightly as thread could be, so that the florets seemed to start from the stem, deceiving the eye at first. In some places this parasite plant had grown up the heath and strangled it, so that the tips turned brown and died. The runners extended in every direction across the ground, like those of strawberries. One creeper had climbed up a bennet, or seeding grass-stalk, binding the stalk and a blade of the grass together, and flowering there. On the ground there were patches of grey lichen; many of the pillar-like stems were crowned with a red top. Under a small boulder stone there was an ants' nest. These boulders, or, as they are called locally, "bowlers," were scattered about the heath. Many of the lesser stones were spotted with dark dots of lichen, not unlike a toad.

Thoughtlessly turning over a boulder about nine inches square, lo! there was subject enough for thinking underneath it—a subject that has been thought about many thousand years; for this piece of rock had formed the roof of an ants' nest. The stone had sunk three inches deep into the dry soil of sand and peaty mould, and in the floor of the hole the ants had worked out their excavations, which resembled an outline map. The largest excavation

was like England; at the top, or north, they had
left a narrow bridge, an eighth of an inch wide, under
which to pass into Scotland, and from Scotland again
another narrow arch led to the Orkney Islands; these
last, however, were dug in the perpendicular side of
the hole. In the corners of these excavations tunnels
ran deeper into the ground, and the ants immediately
began hurrying their treasures, the eggs, down into
these cellars. At one angle a tunnel went beneath
the heath into further excavations beneath a second
boulder stone. Without, a fern grew, and the dead
dry stems of heather crossed each other.

This discovery led to the turning over of another
boulder stone not far off, and under it there appeared
a much more extensive and complete series of galleries,
bridges, cellars and tunnels. In these the whole life-
history of the ant was exposed at a single glance, as
if one had taken off the roofs of a city. One cell
contained a dust-like deposit, another a collection
resembling the dust, but now elongated and a little
greenish; a third treasury, much larger, was piled
up with yellowish grains about the size of wheat,
each with a black dot on the top, and looking like
minute hop-pockets. Besides these, there was a pure
white substance in a corridor, which the irritated
ants seemed particularly anxious to remove out of
sight, and quickly carried away. Among the ants
rushing about there were several with wings; one
took flight; one was seized by a wingless ant and
dragged down into a cellar, as if to prevent its taking
wing. A helpless green fly was in the midst, and
round the outside galleries there crept a creature like

a spider, seeming to try to hide itself. If the nest had been formed under glass, it could not have been more open to view. The stone was carefully replaced.

Below the pine wood on the slope of the hill a plough was already at work, the crop of peas having been harvested. The four horses came up the slope, and at the ridge swept round in a fine curve to go back and open a fresh furrow. As soon as they faced down-hill they paused, well aware of what had to be done, and the ploughman in a manner knocked his plough to pieces, putting it together again the opposite way, that the earth he was about to cut with the share might fall on what he had just turned. With a piece of iron he hammered the edge of the share, to set it, for the hard ground had bent the edge, and it did not cut properly. I said his team looked light; they were not so heavily built as the cart-horses used in many places. No, he said, they did not want heavy horses. "Dese yer thick-boned hosses be more clutter-headed over the clots," as he expressed it, *i.e.* more clumsy or thick-headed over the clods. He preferred comparatively light cart-horses to step well. In the heat of the sun the furze-pods kept popping and bursting open; they are often as full of insects as seeds, which come creeping out. A green and black lady-bird—exactly like a tortoise—flew on to my hand. Again on the heath, and the grass-hoppers rose at every step, sometimes three or four springing in as many directions. They were winged, and as soon as they were up spread their vanes and floated forwards. As the force of the original hop decreased, the wind took their wings and turned them

aside from the straight course before they fell. Down
the dusty road, inches deep in sand, comes a sulphur
butterfly, rushing as quick as if hastening to a butter-
fly-fair. If only rare, how valued he would be! His
colour is so evident and visible; he fills the road,
being brighter than all, and for the moment is more
than the trees and flowers.

Coming so suddenly over the hedge into the road
close to me, he startled me as if I had been awakened
from a dream—I had been thinking it was August,
and woke to find it February—for the sulphur butterfly
is the February pleasure. Between the dark storms
and wintry rains there is a warm sunny interval of
a week in February. Away one goes for a walk, and
presently there appears a bright yellow spot among
the furze, dancing along like a flower let loose. It is
a sulphur butterfly, who thus comes before the earliest
chiffchaff—before the watch begins for the first
swallow. I call it the February pleasure, as each
month has its delight. So associated as this butterfly
is with early spring, to see it again after months
of leaf and flower—after June and July—with the
wheat in shock and the scent of harvest in the land,
is startling. The summer, then, is a dream! It is
still winter; but no, here are the trees in leaf, the
nuts reddening, the hum of bees, and dry summer
dust on the high wiry grass. The sulphur butterfly
comes twice; there is a second brood; but there are
some facts that are always new and surprising,
however well known. I may say again, if only rare,
how this butterfly would be prized! Along the hedgerow there are several spiders' webs. In the centre

they are drawn inwards, forming a funnel, which goes back a few inches into the hedge, and at the bottom of this the spider waits. If you look down the funnel you see his claws at the bottom, ready to run up and seize a fly.

Sitting in the garden after a walk, it is pleasant to watch the eave-swallows feeding their young on the wing. The young bird follows the old one; then they face each other and stay a moment in the air, while the insect food is transferred from beak to beak; with a loud note they part. There was a constant warfare between the eave-swallows and the sparrows frequenting a house where I was staying during the early part of the summer. The sparrows strove their utmost to get possession of the nests the swallows built, and there was no peace between them. It is common enough for one or two swallows' nests to be attacked in this way, but here every nest along the eaves was fought for, and the sparrows succeeded in conquering many of them. The driven-out swallows after a while began to build again, and I noticed that more than a pair seemed to work at the same nest. One nest was worked at by four swallows; often all four came together and twittered at it.

NATURE ON THE ROOF.

INCREASED activity on the housetop marks the approach of spring and summer exactly as in the woods and hedges, for the roof has its migrants, its semi-migrants, and its residents. When the first dandelion is opening on a sheltered bank, and the pale-blue field veronica flowers in the waste corner, the whistle of the starling comes from his favourite ledge. Day by day it is heard more and more, till, when the first green spray appears on the hawthorn, he visits the roof continually. Besides the roof-tree and the chimney-pot, he has his own special place, sometimes under an eave, sometimes between two gables ; and as I sit writing, I can see a pair who have a ledge which slightly projects from the wall between the eave and the highest window. This was made by the builder for an ornament; but my two starlings consider it their own particular possession. They alight with a sort of half-scream half-whistle just over the window, flap their wings, and whistle again, run along the ledge to a spot where there is a gable, and with another note, rise up and enter an aperture between the slates and the wall. There their nest will be in a little time, and busy indeed they will

be when the young require to be fed, to and fro the
fields and the gable the whole day through ; the
busiest and the most useful of birds, for they destroy
thousands upon thousands of insects, and if farmers
were wise, they would never have one shot, no matter
how the thatch was pulled about.

My pair of starlings were frequently at this ledge
last autumn, very late in autumn, and I suspect
they had a winter brood there. The starling does
rear a brood sometimes in the midst of the winter,
contrary as that may seem to our general ideas of
natural history. They may be called roof-residents,
as they visit it all the year round ; they nest in the
roof, rearing two and sometimes three broods ; and
use it as their club and place of meeting. Towards
July the young starlings and those that have for
the time at least finished nesting, flock together, and
pass the day in the fields, returning now and then
to their old home. These flocks gradually increase ;
the starling is so prolific that the flocks become
immense, till in the latter part of the autumn in
southern fields it is common to see a great elm-tree
black with them, from the highest bough downwards,
and the noise of their chattering can be heard a
long distance. They roost in firs or in osier-beds.
But in the blackest days of winter, when frost binds
the ground hard as iron, the starlings return to the
roof almost every day ; they do not whistle much,
but have a peculiar chuckling whistle at the instant
of alighting. In very hard weather, especially snow,
the starlings find it difficult to obtain a living, and
at such times will come to the premises at the rear,

and at farmhouses where cattle are in the yards, search about among them for insects.

The whole history of the starling is interesting, but I must here only mention it as a roof-bird. They are very handsome in their full plumage, which gleams bronze and green among the darker shades; quick in their motions, and full of spirit; loaded to the muzzle with energy, and never still. I hope none of those who are so good as to read what I have written will ever keep a starling in a cage; the cruelty is extreme. As for shooting pigeons at a trap, it is mercy in comparison.

Even before the starling whistles much, the sparrows begin to chirp: in the dead of winter they are silent; but so soon as the warmer winds blow, if only for a day, they begin to chirp. In January this year I used to listen to the sparrows chirping, the starlings whistling, and the chaffinches' "chink, chink" about eight o'clock, or earlier, in the morning: the first two on the roof; the latter, which is not a roof-bird, in some garden shrubs. As the spring advances, the sparrows sing—it is a short song, it is true, but still it is singing—perched at the edge of a sunny wall. There is not a place about the house where they will not build—under the eaves, on the roof, anywhere where there is a projection or shelter, deep in the thatch, under the tiles, in old eave-swallows' nests. The last place I noticed as a favourite one in towns is on the half-bricks left projecting in perpendicular rows at the sides of unfinished houses. Half a dozen nests may be counted at the side of a house on these bricks; and like the starlings, they rear several

broods, and some are nesting late in the autumn.
By degrees as the summer advances they leave the
houses for the corn, and gather in vast flocks, rivalling
those of the starlings. At this time they desert the
roofs, except those who still have nesting duties. In
winter and in the beginning of the new year, they
gradually return; migration thus goes on under the
eyes of those who care to notice it. In London, some
who fed sparrows on the roof found that rooks also
came for the crumbs placed out. I sometimes see
a sparrow chasing a rook, as if angry, and trying
to drive it away over the roofs where I live. The
thief does not retaliate, but, like a thief, flees from
the scene of his guilt. This is not only in the
breeding season, when the rook steals eggs, but in
winter. Town residents are apt to despise the
sparrow, seeing him always black; but in the country
the sparrows are as clean as a pink; and in themselves they are the most animated, clever little
creatures.

They are easily tamed. The Parisians are fond
of taming them. At a certain hour in the Tuileries
Gardens, you may see a man perfectly surrounded
with a crowd of sparrows—some perching on his
shoulder; some fluttering in the air immediately
before his face; some on the ground like a tribe
of followers; and others on the marble seats. He
jerks a crumb of bread into the air—a sparrow dexterously seizes it as he would a flying insect; he
puts a crumb between his lips—a sparrow takes it
out and feeds from his mouth. Meantime they keep
up a constant chirping; those that are satisfied still

stay by and adjust their feathers. He walks on, giving a little chirp with his mouth, and they follow him along the path—a cloud about his shoulders, and the rest flying from shrub to shrub, perching, and then following again. They are all perfectly clean—a contrast to the London sparrow. I came across one of these sparrow-tamers by chance, and was much amused at the scene, which, to any one not acquainted with birds, appears marvellous; but it is really as simple as possible, and you can repeat it for yourself if you have patience, for they are so sharp they soon understand you. They seem to play at nest-making before they really begin; taking up straws in their beaks, and carrying them half-way to the roof, then letting the straws float away; and the same with stray feathers. Neither of these, starlings nor sparrows, seem to like the dark. Under the roof, between it and the first ceiling, there is a large open space; if the slates or tiles are kept in good order, very little light enters, and this space is nearly dark in daylight. Even if chinks admit a beam of light, it is not enough; they seldom enter or fly about there, though quite accessible to them. But if the roof is in bad order, and this space light, they enter freely. Though nesting in holes, yet they like light. The swallows could easily go in and make nests upon the beams, but they will not, unless the place is well lit. They do not like darkness in the daytime.

The swallows bring us the sunbeams on their wings from Africa to fill the fields with flowers. From the time of the arrival of the first swallow the flowers take heart; the few and scanty plants that had braved the earlier cold are succeeded by a constantly enlarging list, till the banks and lanes are full of them. The chimney-swallow is usually the fore-runner of the three house-swallows; and perhaps no fact in natural history has been so much studied as the migration of these tender birds. The commonest things are always the most interesting. In summer there is no bird so common everywhere as the swallow, and for that reason, many overlook it, though they rush to see a "white" elephant. But the deepest thinkers have spent hours and hours in con-sidering the problem of the swallow—its migrations, its flight, its habits; great poets have loved it; great artists and art-writers have curiously studied it. The idea that it is necessary to seek the wilderness or the thickest woods for nature is a total mistake; nature is at home, on the roof, close to every one. Eave-swallows, or house-martins (easily distinguished by the white bar across the tail), build sometimes in the shelter of the porches of old houses.

As you go in or out, the swallows visiting or leaving their nests fly so closely as almost to brush the face. Swallow means porch-bird, and for centuries and centuries their nests have been placed in the closest proximity to man. They might be called man's birds, so attached are they to the human race. I think the greatest ornament a house can have is the nest of an eave-swallow under the eaves—far superior to the most elaborate carving, colouring, or arrange-ment the architect can devise. There is no ornament like the swallow's nest; the home of a messenger

between man and the blue heavens, between us and
the sunlight, and all the promise of the sky.   The
joy of life, the highest and tenderest feelings, thoughts
that soar on the swallow's wings, come to the round
nest under the roof.   Not only to-day, not only the
hopes of future years, but all the past dwells there.
Year after year the generations and descent of the
swallow have been associated with our homes, and
all the events of successive lives have taken place
under their guardianship.   The swallow is the genius
of good to a house.   Let its nest, then, stay; to
me it seems the extremity of barbarism, or rather
stupidity, to knock it down.   I wish I could induce
them to build under the eaves of this house; I would
if I could discover some means of communicating
with them.

It is a peculiarity of the swallow that you cannot
make it afraid of you; just the reverse of other
birds.   The swallow does not understand being
repulsed, but comes back again.   Even knocking
the nest down will not drive it away, until the
stupid process has been repeated several years.   The
robin must be coaxed; the sparrow is suspicious, and
though easy to tame, quick to notice the least alarm-
ing movement.   The swallow will not be driven away.
He has not the slightest fear of man; he flies to
his nest close to the window, under the low eave,
or on the beams in the out-houses, no matter if you
are looking on or not.   Bold as the starlings are,
they will seldom do this.   But in the swallow,
the instinct of suspicion is reversed; an instinct of
confidence occupies its place.   In addition to the

eave-swallow, to which I have chiefly alluded, and the chimney-swallow, there is the swift, also a roof-bird, and making its nest in the slates of houses in the midst of towns. These three are migrants in the fullest sense, and come to our houses over thousands of miles of land and sea.

Robins frequently visit the roof for insects, especially when it is thatched; so do wrens; and the latter, after they have peered along, have a habit of perching at the extreme angle of á gable, or the extreme edge of a corner, and uttering their song. Finches occasionally fly up to the roofs of country-houses if shrubberies are near, also in pursuit of insects; but they are not truly roof-birds. Wagtails perch on roofs; they often have their nests in the ivy, or creepers trained against walls; they are quite at home, and are frequently seen on the ridges of farmhouses. Tits of several species, particularly the great titmouse and the blue tit, come to thatch for insects, both in summer and winter. In some districts where they are common, it is not unusual to see a goatsucker or fern-owl hawk along close to the eaves in the dusk of the evening for moths. The white owl is a roof-bird (though not often of the house), building inside the roof, and sitting there all day in some shaded corner. They do sometimes take up their residence in the roofs of outhouses attached to dwellings, but not often nowadays, though still residing in the roofs of old castles. Jackdaws, again, are roof-birds, building in the roofs of towers. Bats live in roofs, and hang there wrapped up in their membranous wings till the evening calls them forth. They are residents in the full sense, remaining all the year round, though principally seen in the warmer months; but they are there in the colder, hidden away, and if the temperature rises, will venture out and hawk to and fro in the midst of the winter. Tame pigeons and doves hardly come into this paper, but still it is their habit to use roofs as tree-tops. Rats and mice creep through the crevices of roofs, and in old country-houses hold a sort of nightly carnival, racing to and fro under the roof. Weasels sometimes follow them indoors and up to their roof strongholds.

When the first warm rays of spring sunshine strike against the southern side of the chimney, sparrows perch there and enjoy it; and again in autumn, when the general warmth of the atmosphere is declining, they still find a little pleasant heat there. They make use of the radiation of heat, as the gardener does who trains his fruit-trees to a wall. Before the autumn has thinned the leaves, the swallows gather on the highest ridge of the roof in a row and twitter to each other; they know the time is approaching when they must depart for another climate. In winter, many birds seek the thatched roofs to roost. Wrens, tits, and even blackbirds roost in the holes left by sparrows or starlings.

Every crevice is the home of insects, or used by them for the deposit of their eggs—under the tiles or slates, where mortar has dropped out between the bricks, in the holes of thatch, and on the straws. The number of insects that frequent a large roof must be very great—all the robins, wrens, bats, and so on, can scarcely affect them; nor the spiders, though these, too, are numerous. Then there are the moths, and those creeping creatures that work out of sight, boring their way through the rafters and beams. Sometimes a sparrow may be seen clinging to the bare wall of the house; tits do the same thing. It is surprising how they manage to hold on. They are taking insects from the apertures of the mortar. Where the slates slope to the south, the sunshine soon heats them, and passing butterflies alight on the warm surface, and spread out their wings, as if hovering over the heat. Flies are attracted in crowds sometimes to heated slates and tiles, and wasps will occasionally pause there. Wasps are addicted to haunting houses, and, in the autumn, feed on the flies. Floating germs carried by the air must necessarily lodge in numbers against roofs; so do dust and invisible particles; and together, these make the rain-water collected in water-butts after a storm turbid and dark; and it soon becomes full of living organisms.

Lichen and moss grow on the mortar wherever it has become slightly disintegrated; and if any mould, however minute, by any means accumulates between the slates, there, too, they spring up, and even on the slates themselves. Tiles are often coloured yellow by such growths. On some old roofs, which have decayed, and upon which detritus has accumulated, wallflowers may be found; and the house-leek takes capricious root where it fancies. The stonecrop is the finest of roof-plants, sometimes forming a, broad patch of brilliant yellow. Birds carry up seeds and grains, and these germinate in moist thatch. Groundsel, for instance, and stray stalks of wheat, thin and drooping for lack of soil, are sometimes seen there, besides grasses. Ivy is familiar as a roof-creeper. Some ferns and the pennywort will grow on the wall close to the roof. A correspondent tells me that in Wales he found a cottage perfectly roofed with fern—it grew so thickly as to conceal the roof. Had a painter put this in a picture, many would have exclaimed: "How fanciful! He must have made it up; it could never have grown like that!" Not long after receiving my correspondent's kind letter, I chanced to find a roof near London upon which the same fern was growing in lines along the tiles. It grew plentifully, but was not in so flourishing a condition as that found in Wales. Painters are sometimes accused of calling upon their imagination when they are really depicting fact, for the ways of nature vary very much in different localities, and that which may seem impossible in one place is common enough in another.

Where will not ferns grow? We saw one attached to the under-side of a glass coal-hole cover; its green could be seen through the thick glass on which people stepped daily.

Recently, much attention has been paid to the dust which is found on roofs and ledges at great heights. This meteoric dust, as it is called, consists of minute particles of iron, which are thought to fall from the highest part of the atmosphere, or possibly to be attracted to the earth from space. Lightning usually strikes the roof. The whole subject of lightning-conductors has been re-opened of late years, there being reason to think that mistakes have been made in the manner of their erection. The reason English roofs are high-pitched is not only because of the rain, that it may shoot off quickly, but on account of snow. Once now and then there comes a snow-year, and those who live in houses with flat surfaces anywhere on the roof soon discover how inconvenient they are. The snow is sure to find its way through, damaging ceilings, and doing other mischief. Sometimes, in fine summer weather, people remark how pleasant it would be if the roof were flat, so that it could be used as a terrace, as it is in warmer climates. But the fact is, the English roof, although now merely copied and repeated without a thought of the reason of its shape, grew up from experience of severe winters. Of old, great care and ingenuity—what we should now call artistic skill—were employed in constructing the roof. It was not only pleasant to the eye with its gables, but the woodwork was wonderfully well done. Such roofs may still be seen on ancient mansions, having endured for centuries. They are splendid pieces of workmanship, and seen from afar among foliage, are admired by every one who has the least taste. Draughtsmen and painters value them highly. No matter whether reproduced on a large canvas or in a little woodcut, their proportions please. The roof is much neglected in modern houses; it is either conventional, or it is full indeed of gables, but gables that do not agree, as it were, with each other —that are obviously put there on purpose to look artistic, and fail altogether. Now, the ancient roofs were true works of art, consistent, and yet each varied to its particular circumstances, and each impressed

with the individuality of the place and of the designer.
The finest old roofs were built of oak or chestnut; the
beams are black with age, and, in that condition, oak
is scarcely distinguishable from chestnut.

So the roof has its natural history, its science, and
art; it has its seasons, its migrants and residents, of
whom a housetop calendar might be made. The fine
old roofs which have just been mentioned are often
associated with historic events and the rise of
families; and the roof-tree, like the hearth, has a
range of proverbs or sayings and ancient lore to itself.
More than one great monarch has been slain by a tile
thrown from the housetop, and numerous other inci-
dents have occurred in connection with it. The most
interesting is the story of the Grecian mother who,
with her infant, was on the roof, when, in a moment
of inattention, the child crept to the edge, and was
balanced on the very verge. To call to it, to touch
it, would have insured its destruction; but the
mother, without a second's thought, bared her breast,
and the child eagerly turning to it, was saved!

ONE OF THE NEW VOTERS.

I.

IF any one were to get up about half-past five on
an August morning and look out of an eastern
window in the country, he would see the distant trees
almost hidden by a white mist. The tops of the
larger groups of elms would appear above it, and
by these the line of the hedgerows could be traced.
Tier after tier they stretch along, rising by degrees
on a gentle slope, the space between filled with haze.
Whether there were corn-fields or meadows under this
white cloud he could not tell—a cloud that might
have come down from the sky, leaving it a clear
azure. This morning haze means intense heat in
the day. It is hot already, very hot, for the sun
is shining with all his strength, and if you wish
the house to be cool it is time to set the sunblinds.

Roger, the reaper, had slept all night in the cowhouse, lying on the raised platform of narrow planks
put up for cleanliness when the cattle were there.
He had set the wooden window wide open and left
the door ajar when he came stumbling in overnight,
long after the late swallows had settled in their nests
on the beams, and the bats had wearied of moth
catching. One of the swallows twittered a little,

as much as to say to his mate, "My love, it is only
a reaper, we need not be afraid," and all was silence
and darkness. Roger did not so much as take off his
boots, but flung himself on the boards crash, curled
himself up hedgehog fashion with some old sacks,
and immediately began to breathe heavily. He had
no difficulty in sleeping, first because his muscles
had been tried to the utmost, and next because his
skin was full to the brim, not of jolly "good ale
and old," but of the very smallest and poorest of
wish-washy beer. In his own words, it "blowed
him up till he very nigh bust." Now the great
authorities on dyspepsia, so eagerly studied by the
wealthy folk whose stomachs are deranged, tell us
that a very little flatulence will make the heart beat
irregularly and cause the most distressing symptoms.

Roger had swallowed at least a gallon of a liquid
chemically designed, one might say, on purpose to
utterly upset the internal economy. Harvest beer
is probably the vilest drink in the world. The men
say it is made by pouring muddy water into empty
casks returned sour from use, and then brushing
them round and round inside with a besom. This
liquid leaves a stickiness on the tongue and a harsh
feeling at the back of the mouth which soon turns
to thirst, so that having once drunk a pint the
drinker must go on drinking. The peculiar dryness
caused by this beer is not like any other throat
drought—worse than dust, or heat, or thirst from
work; there is no satisfying it. With it there go
down the germs of fermentation, a sour, yeasty, and,
as it were, secondary fermentation; not that kind

which is necessary to make beer, but the kind that
unmakes and spoils beer. It is beer rotting and
decomposing in the stomach. Violent diarrhœa
often follows, and then the exhaustion thus caused
induces the men to drink more in order to regain
the strength necessary to do their work. The great
heat of the sun and the heat of hard labour, the
strain and perspiration, of course try the body and
weaken the digestion. To distend the stomach with
half a gallon of this liquor, expressly compounded
to ferment, is about the most murderous thing a
man could do—murderous because it exposes him
to the risk of sunstroke. So vile a drink there is
not elsewhere in the world; arrack, and potato-spirit,
and all the other killing extracts of the distiller are
not equal to it. Upon this abominable mess the
golden harvest of English fields is gathered in.

Some people have in consequence endeavoured to
induce the harvesters to accept a money payment
in place of beer, and to a certain extent successfully.
Even then, however, they must drink something.
Many manage on weak tea after a fashion, but not
so well as the abstainers would have us think.
Others have brewed for their men a miserable
stuff in buckets, an infusion of oatmeal, and got a
few to drink it; but English labourers will never
drink oatmeal-water unless they are paid to do it.
If they are paid extra beer-money and oatmeal-
water is made for them gratis, some will, of course,
imbibe it, especially if they see that thereby they
may obtain little favours from their employer by
yielding to his fad. By drinking the crotchet perhaps

they may get a present now and then—food for themselves, cast-off clothes for their families, and so on.
For it is a remarkable feature of human natural
history, the desire to proselytize. The spectacle of
John Bull—jovial John Bull—offering his men a
bucket of oatmeal liquor is not a pleasant one. Such
a John Bull ought to be ashamed of himself.

The truth is the English farmer's man was and
is, and will be, a drinker of beer. Neither tea,
nor oatmeal, nor vinegar and water (coolly recom-
mended by indoor folk) will do for him. His natural
constitution rebels against such " peevish " drink.
In winter he wants beer against the cold and the
frosty rime and the heavy raw mist that hangs about
the hollows ; in spring and autumn against the rain,
and in summer to support him under the pressure
of additional work and prolonged hours. Those who
really wish well to the labourer cannot do better than
see that he really has beer to drink—real beer,
genuine brew of malt and hops, a moderate quantity
of which will supply force to his thews and sinews,
and will not intoxicate or injure. If by giving him a
small money payment in lieu of such large quantities
you can induce him to be content with a little, so much
the better. If an employer followed that plan, and at
the same time once or twice a day sent out a moderate
supply of genuine beer as a gift to his men, he would
do them all the good in the world, and at the same
time obtain for himself their goodwill and hearty
assistance, that hearty work which is worth so much.

Roger breathed heavily in his sleep in the cowhouse, because the vile stuff he had taken puffed

him up and obstructed nature. The tongue in his
open mouth became parched and cracked, swollen
and dry; he slept indeed, but he did not rest; he
groaned heavily at times and rolled aside. Once
he awoke choking—he could not swallow, his tongue
was so dry and large; he sat up, swore, and again
lay down. The rats in the sties had already discovered that a man slept in the cowhouse, a place
they rarely visited, as there was nothing there to eat;
how they found it out no one knows. They are clever
creatures, the despised rats. They came across in
the night and looked under his bed, supposing that
he might have eaten his bread-and-cheese for supper
there, and that fragments might have dropped between
the boards. There were none. They mounted the
boards and sniffed round him; they would have
stolen the food from his very pocket if it had been
there. Nor could they find a bundle in a handkerchief, which they would have gnawn through
speedily. Not a scrap of food was there to be smelt
at, so they left him. Roger had indeed gone supper-
less, as usual; his supper he had swilled and not
eaten. His own fault; he should have exercised
self-control. Well, I don't know; let us consider
further before we judge.

In houses the difficulty often is to get the servants
up in the morning; one cannot wake, and the rest
sleep too sound—much the same thing; yet they
have clocks and alarums. The reapers are never
behind. Roger got off his planks, shook himself,
went outside the shed, and tightened his shoelaces
in the bright light. His rough hair he just pushed

back from his forehead, and that was his toilet. His dry throat sent him to the pump, but he did not swallow much of the water—he washed his mouth out, and that was enough; and so without breakfast he went to his work. Looking down from the stile on the high ground there seemed to be a white cloud resting on the valley, through which the tops of the high trees penetrated; the hedgerows beneath were concealed, and their course could only be traced by the upper branches of the elms. Under this cloud the wheat-fields were blotted out; there seemed neither corn nor grass, work for man nor food for animal; there could be nothing doing there surely. In the stillness of the August morning, without song of bird, the sun, shining brilliantly high above the mist, seemed to be the only living thing, to possess the whole and reign above absolute peace. It is a curious sight to see the early harvest morn—all hushed under the burning sun, a morn that you know is full of life and meaning, yet quiet as if man's foot had never trodden the land. Only the sun is there, rolling on his endless way.

Roger's head was bound with brass, but had it not been he would not have observed anything in the aspect of the earth. Had a brazen band been drawn firmly round his forehead it could not have felt more stupefied. His eyes blinked in the sunlight; every now and then he stopped to save himself from staggering; he was not in a condition to think. It would have mattered not at all if his head had been clear; earth, sky, and sun were nothing to him; he knew the footpath, and saw that the day would be fine and hot, and that was sufficient for him, because his eyes had never been opened.

The reaper had risen early to his labour, but the birds had preceded him hours. Before the sun was up the swallows had left their beams in the cowshed and twittered out into the air. The rooks and wood-pigeons and doves had gone to the corn, the blackbird to the stream, the finch to the hedgerow, the bees to the heath on the hills, the humble-bees to the clover in the plain. Butterflies rose from the flowers by the footpath, and fluttered before him to and fro and round and back again to the place whence they had been driven. Gold-finches tasting the first thistledown rose from the corner where the thistles grew thickly. A hundred sparrows came rushing up into the hedge, suddenly filling the boughs with brown fruit; they chirped and quarrelled in their talk, and rushed away again back to the corn as he stepped nearer. The boughs were stripped of their winged brown berries as quickly as they had grown. Starlings ran before the cows feeding in the aftermath, so close to their mouths as to seem in danger of being licked up by their broad tongues. All creatures, from the tiniest insect upward, were in reality busy under that curtain of white-heat haze. It looked so still, so quiet, from afar; entering it and passing among the fields, all that lived was found busy at its long day's work. Roger did not interest himself in these things, in the wasps that left the gate as he approached— they were making *papier-maché* from the wood of the top bar,—in the bright poppies brushing against his drab unpolished boots, in the hue of the wheat or the white convolvulus; they were nothing to him.

Why should they be? His life was work without skill or thought, the work of the horse, of the crane that lifts stones and timber. His food was rough, his drink rougher, his lodging dry planks. His books were—none; his picture-gallery a coloured print at the alehouse—a dog, dead, by a barrel, "Trust is dead; Bad Pay killed him." Of thought he thought nothing; of hope his idea was a shilling a week more wages; of any future for himself of comfort such as even a good cottage can give—of any future whatever—he had no more conception than the horse in the shafts of the waggon. A human animal simply in all this, yet if you reckoned upon him as simply an animal—as has been done these centuries—you would now be mistaken. But why should he note the colour of the butterfly, the bright light of the sun, the hue of the wheat? This loveli-ness gave him no cheese for breakfast; of beauty in itself, for itself, he had no idea. How should he? To many of us the harvest—the summer—is a time of joy in light and colour; to him it was a time for adding yet another crust of hardness to the thick skin of his hands.

Though the haze looked like a mist it was per-fectly dry; the wheat was as dry as noon; not a speck of dew, and the pimpernels wide open for a burning day. The reaping-machine began to rattle as he came up, and work was ready for him. At breakfast-time his fellows lent him a quarter of a loaf, some young onions, and a drink from their

tea. He ate little, and the tea slipped from his hot
tongue like water from the bars of a grate; his
tongue was like the heated iron the housemaid tries
before using it on the linen. As the reaping-machine
went about the gradually decreasing square of corn,
narrowing it by a broad band each time, the wheat
fell flat on the short stubble. Roger stooped, and,
gathering sufficient together, took a few straws,
knotted them to another handful as you might tie
two pieces of string, and twisted the band round
the sheaf. He worked stooping to gather the wheat,
bending to tie it in sheaves; stooping, bending—
stooping, bending,—and so across the field. Upon
his head and back the fiery sun poured down the
ceaseless and increasing heat of the August day.
His face grew red, his neck black; the drought of
the dry ground rose up and entered his mouth and
nostrils, a warm air seemed to rise from the earth
and fill his chest. His body ached from the ferment
of the vile beer, his back ached with stooping, his
forehead was bound tight with a brazen band. They
brought some beer at last; it was like the spring in
the desert to him. The vicious liquor—"a hair of
the dog that bit him"—sank down his throat,
grateful and refreshing to his disordered palate as
if he had drunk the very shadow of green boughs.
Good ale would have seemed nauseous to him at that
moment, his taste and stomach destroyed by so many
gallons of this. He was "pulled together," and
worked easier; the slow hours went on, and it was
luncheon. He could have borrowed more food, but
he was content instead with a screw of tobacco for
his pipe and his allowance of beer.

They sat in the corner of the field. There were no trees for shade; they had been cut down as injurious to corn, but there were a few maple bushes and thin ash sprays, which seemed better than the open. The bushes cast no shade at all, the sun being so nearly overhead, but they formed a kind of enclosure, an open-air home, for men seldom sit down if they can help it on the bare and level plain; they go to the bushes, to the corner, or even to some hollow. It is not really any advantage; it is habit; or shall we not rather say that it is nature? Brought back as it were in the open field to the primitive conditions of life, they resumed the same instincts that controlled man in the ages past. Ancient man sought the shelter of trees and banks, of caves and hollows, and so the labourers under somewhat the same conditions came to the corner where the bushes grew. There they left their coats and slung up their luncheon-bundles to the branches; there the children played and took charge of the infants; there the women had their hearth and hung their kettle over a fire of sticks.

II.

In August the unclouded sun, when there is no wind, shines as fervently in the harvest-field as in Spain. It is doubtful if the Spanish people feel the heat so much as our reapers; they have their siesta; their habits have become attuned to the sun, and it is no special strain upon them. In India our troops are carefully looked after in the hot weather, and everything made as easy for them as possible; without care and special clothing and coverings for the head they could not long endure. The English simoon of heat drops suddenly on the heads of the harvesters and finds them entirely unprepared; they have not so much as a cooling drink ready; they face it, as it were, unarmed. The sun spares not; it is fire from morn till night. Afar in the town the sunblinds are up, there is a tent on the lawn in the shade, people drink claret-cup and use ice; ice has never been seen in the harvest-field. Indoors they say they are melting lying on a sofa in a darkened room, made dusky to keep out the heat. The fire falls straight from the sky on the heads of the harvesters—men, women, and children—and the white-hot light beats up again from the dry straw and the hard ground.

The tender flowers endure; the wide petal of the poppy, which withers between the fingers, lies afloat on the air as the lilies on water, afloat and open to the weight of the heat. The red pimpernel looks straight up at the sky from the early morning till its hour of closing in the afternoon. Pale blue speedwell does not fade; the pale blue stands the warmth equally with the scarlet. Far in the thick wheat the streaked convolvulus winds up the stalks, and is not smothered for want of air though wrapped and circled with corn. Beautiful though they are, they are bloodless, not sensitive; we have given to them our feelings, they do not share our pain or pleasure. Heat has gone into the hollow stalks of the wheat and down the yellow tubes to the roots, drying them in the earth. Heat has dried the leaves upon the hedge, and they touch rough—dusty rough, as books touch that have been lying unused; the plants on the bank are drying

up and turning white. Heat has gone down into the
cracks of the ground; the bar of the stile is so dry
and powdery in the crevices that if a reaper chanced
to drop a match on it there would seem risk of fire.
The still atmosphere is laden with heat, and does not
move in the corner of the field between the bushes.

Roger the reaper smoked out his tobacco; the
children played round and watched for scraps of food;
the women complained of the heat; the men said
nothing. It is seldom that a labourer grumbles much
at the weather, except as interfering with his work.
Let the heat increase, so it would only keep fine.
The fire in the sky meant money. Work went on
again; Roger had now to go to another field to pitch
—that is, help to load the waggon; as a young man,
that was one of the jobs allotted to him. This was
the reverse. Instead of stooping he had now to strain
himself upright and lift sheaves over his head. His
stomach empty of everything but small ale did not
like this any more than his back had liked the other;
but those who work for bare food must not question
their employment. Heavily the day drove on; there
was more beer, and again more beer, because it was
desired to clear some fields that evening. Mono-
tonously pitching the sheaves, Roger laboured by the
waggon till the last had been loaded—till the moon
was shining. His brazen forehead was unbound now;
in spite of the beer the work and the perspiration had
driven off the aching. He was weary but well. Nor
had he been dull during the day; he had talked and
joked—cumbrously in labourers' fashion—with his
fellows. His aches, his empty stomach, his labour,

and the heat had not evercome the vitality of his spirits. There was life enough left for a little rough play as the group gathered together and passed out through the gateway. Life enough left in him to go with the rest to the alehouse; and what else, oh moralist, would you have done in his place? This, remember, is not a fancy sketch of rural poetry; this is the reaper's real existence.

He had been in the harvest-field fourteen hours, exposed to the intense heat, not even shielded by a pith helmet; he had worked the day through with thew and sinew; he had had for food a little dry bread and a few onions, for drink a little weak tea and a great deal of small beer. The moon was now shining in the sky, still bright with sunset colours. Fourteen hours of sun and labour and hard fare! Now tell him what to do. To go straight to his plank-bed in the cowhouse; to eat a little more dry bread, borrow some cheese or greasy bacon, munch it alone, and sit musing till sleep came—he who had nothing to muse about. I think it would need a very clever man indeed to invent something for him to do, some way for him to spend his evening. Read! To recommend a man to read after fourteen hours burning sun is indeed a mockery; darn his stockings would be better. There really is nothing whatsoever that the cleverest and most benevolent person could suggest. Before any benevolent or well-meaning suggestions could be effective the preceding circumstances must be changed—the hours and conditions of labour, everything; and can that be done? The world has been working these thousands of years, and

still it is the same; with our engines, our electric
light, our printing press, still the coarse labour of the
mine, the quarry, the field has to be carried out by
human hands. While that is so, it is useless to
recommend the weary reaper to read. For a man is
not a horse : the horse's day's work is over; taken to
his stable he is content, his mind goes no deeper than
the bottom of his manger, and so long as his nose
does not feel the wood, so long as it is met by corn
and hay, he will endure happily. But Roger the
reaper is not a horse.

Just as his body needed food and drink, so did his
mind require recreation, and that chiefly consists of
conversation. The drinking and the smoking are in
truth but the attributes of the labourer's public-house
evening. It is conversation that draws him thither,
just as it draws men with money in their pockets to the
club and the houses of their friends. Any one can
drink or smoke alone; it needs several for conversation,
for company. You pass a public-house—the reaper's
house—in the summer evening. You see a number of
men grouped about trestle-tables out of doors, and
others sitting at the open window; there is an odour of
tobacco, a chink of glasses and mugs. You can smell
the tobacco and see the ale; you cannot see the indefinite power which holds men there—the magnetism of
company and conversation. *Their* conversation, not
your conversation; not the last book, the last play;
not saloon conversation; but theirs—talk in which
neither you nor any one of your condition could really
join. To us there would seem nothing at all in that
conversation, vapid and subjectless; to them it means

much. We have not been through the same circumstances: our day has been differently spent, and the
same words have therefore a varying value. Certain
it is, that it is conversation that takes men to the
public-house. Had Roger been a horse he would
have hastened to borrow some food, and, having eaten
that, would have cast himself at once upon his rude
bed. Not being an animal, though his life and work
were animal, he went with his friends to talk. Let
none unjustly condemn him as a blackguard for that
—no, not even though they had seen him at ten
o'clock unsteadily walking to his shed, and guiding
himself occasionally with his hands to save himself
from stumbling. He blundered against the door, and
the noise set the swallows on the beams twittering.
He reached his bedstead, and sat down and tried to
unlace his boots, but could not. He threw himself
upon the sacks and fell asleep. Such was one twenty-
four hours of harvest-time.

The next and the next, for weeks, were almost
exactly similar; now a little less beer, now a little
more; now tying up, now pitching, now cutting a
small field or corner with a fagging-hook. Once now
and then there was a great supper at the farm. Once
he fell out with another fellow, and they had a fight;
Roger, however, had had so much ale, and his oppo-
nent so much whisky, that their blows were soft and
helpless. They both fell—that is, they stumbled,
—they were picked up, there was some more beer,
and it was settled. One afternoon Roger became
suddenly giddy, and was so ill that he did no more
work that day, and very little on the following. It

was something like a sunstroke, but fortunately a slight attack; on the third day he resumed his place. Continued labour in the sun, little food and much drink, stomach derangement, in short, accounted for his illness. Though he resumed his place and worked on, he was not so well afterwards; the work was more of an effort to him, and his face lost its fulness, and became drawn and pointed. Still he laboured, and would not miss an hour, for harvest was coming to an end, and the extra wages would soon cease. For the first week or so of haymaking or reaping the men usually get drunk, delighted with the prospect before them, then they settle down fairly well. Towards the end they struggle hard to recover lost time and the money spent in ale.

As the last week approached, Roger went up into the village and ordered the shoemaker to make him a good pair of boots. He paid partly for them then, and the rest next pay-day. This was a tremendous effort. The labourer usually pays a shilling at a time, but Roger mistrusted himself. Harvest was practically over, and after all the labour and the long hours, the exposure to the sun and the rude lodging, he found he should scarcely have thirty shillings. With the utmost ordinary care he could have saved a good lump of money. He was a single man, and his actual keep cost but little. Many married labourers, who had been forced by hard necessity to economy, contrived to put by enough to buy clothes for their families. The single man, with every advantage, hardly had thirty shillings, and even then it showed extraordinary prudence on his part to go and purchase a pair of

boots for the winter. Very few in his place would
have been as thoughtful as that; they would have
got boots somehow in the end, but not beforehand.
This life of animal labour does not grow the spirit
of economy. Not only in farming, but in navvy work,
in the rougher work of factories and mines, the same
fact is evident. The man who labours with thew and
sinew at horse labour—crane labour—not for himself,
but for others, is not the man who saves. If he
worked for his own hand possibly he might, no
matter how rough his labour and fare; not while
working for another. Roger reached his distant
home among the meadows at last, with one golden
half-sovereign in his pocket. That and his new pair
of boots, not yet finished, represented the golden
harvest to him. He lodged with his parents when at
home; he was so far fortunate that he had a bed to
go to; therefore in the estimation of his class he was
not badly off. But if we consider his position as
regards his own life we must recognize that he was
very badly off indeed, so much precious time and the
strength of his youth having been wasted.

Often it is stated that the harvest wages recoup
the labourer for the low weekly receipts of the year,
and if the money be put down in figures with pen and
ink it is so. But in actual fact the pen-and-ink figures
do not represent the true case; these extra figures
have been paid for, and gold may be bought too
dear. Roger had paid heavily for his half-sovereign
and his boots; his pinched face did not look as if he
had benefited greatly. His cautious old father, rendered frugal by forty years of labour, had done fairly

well; the young man not at all. The old man, having a cottage, in a measure worked for his own hand. The young man, with none but himself to think of, scattered his money to the winds. Is money earned with such expenditure of force worth the having? Look at the arm of a woman labouring in the harvest-field—thin, muscular, sinewy, black almost, it tells of continual strain. After much of this she becomes pulled out of shape, the neck loses its roundness and shows the sinews, the chest flattens. In time the women find the strain of it tell severely. I am not trying to make out a case of special hardship, being aware that both men, women, and children work as hard and perhaps suffer more in cities; I am simply describing the realities of rural life behind the scenes. The golden harvest is the first scene; the golden wheat, glorious under the summer sun. Bright poppies flower in its depths, and convolvulus climbs the stalks. Butterflies float slowly over the yellow surface as they might over a lake of colour. To linger by it, to visit it day by day, at even to watch the sunset by it, and see it pale under the changing light, is a delight to the thoughtful mind. There is so much in the wheat, there are books of meditation in it, it is dear to the heart. Behind these beautiful aspects comes the reality of human labour—hours upon hours of heat and strain; there comes the reality of a rude life, and in the end little enough of gain. The wheat is beautiful, but human life is labour.

THE MODERN THAMES.

I.

THE wild red deer can never again come down to drink
at the Thames in the dusk of the evening as once
they did. While modern civilization endures, the
larger fauna must necessarily be confined to parks
or restrained to well-marked districts; but for that
very reason the lesser creatures of the wood, the field,
and the river should receive the more protection. If
this applies to the secluded country, far from the stir
of cities, still more does it apply to the neighbourhood
of London. From a sportsman's point of view, or from
that of a naturalist, the state of the river is one of
chaos. There is no order. The Thames appears free
even from the usual rules which are in force upon
every highway. A man may not fire a gun within a
certain distance of a road under a penalty—a law
enacted for the safety of passengers, who were formerly
endangered by persons shooting small birds along the
hedges bordering roads. Nor may he shoot at all,
not so much as fire off a pistol (as recently publicly
proclaimed by the Metropolitan police to restrain the
use of revolvers), without a licence. But on the river
people do as they choose, and there does not seem to

be any law at all—or at least there is no authority to
enforce it, if it exists. Shooting from boats and from
the towing-path is carried on in utter defiance of the
licensing law, of the game law (as applicable to wild
fowl), and of the safety of persons who may be passing.
The moorhens are shot, the kingfishers have been
nearly exterminated or driven away from some parts,
the once common black-headed bunting is comparatively scarce in the more frequented reaches,
and if there is nothing else to shoot at, then the
swallows are slaughtered. Some have even taken to
shooting at the rooks in the trees or fields by the
river with small-bore rifles—a most dangerous thing
to do. The result is that the osier-beds on the eyots
and by the backwaters—the copses of the river—are
almost devoid of life. A few moorhens creep under
the aquatic grasses and conceal themselves beneath
the bushes, water-voles hide among the flags, but the
once extensive host of water-fowl and river life has
been reduced to the smallest limits. Water-fowl
cannot breed because they are shot on the nest, or
their eggs taken. As for rarer birds, of course they
have not the slightest chance.

The fish have fared better because they have received the benefit of close seasons, enforced with more
or less vigilance all along the river. They are also
protected by regulations making it illegal to capture
them except in a sportsmanlike manner; snatching,
for instance, is unlawful. Riverside proprietors preserve some reaches, piscatorial societies preserve others,
and the complaint indeed is that the rights of the
public have been encroached upon. The too exclusive

preservation of fish is in a measure responsible for the destruction of water-fowl, which are cleared off preserved places in order that they may not help themselves to fry or spawn. On the other hand, the societies may claim to have saved parts of the river from being entirely deprived of fish, for it is not long since it appeared as if the stream would be quite cleared out. Large quantities of fish have also been placed in the river taken from ponds and bodily transported to the Thames. So that upon the whole the fish have been well looked after of recent years.

The more striking of the aquatic plants—such as white water-lilies—have been much diminished in quantity by the constant plucking, and injury is said to have been done by careless navigation. In things of this kind a few persons can do a great deal of damage. Two or three men with guns, and indifferent to the interests of sport or natural history, at work every day, can clear a long stretch of river of water-fowl, by scaring if not by actually killing them. Imagine three or four such gentry allowed to wander at will in a large game preserve—in a week they would totally destroy it as a preserve. The river, after all, is but a narrow band as it were, and is easily commanded by a gun. So, too, with fish poachers; a very few men with nets can quickly empty a good piece of water: and flowers like water-lilies, which grow only in certain spots, are soon pulled or spoiled. This aspect of the matter—the immense mischief which can be effected by a very few persons—should be carefully borne in mind in framing any regulations. For the mischief done on

the river is really the work of a small number, a mere
fraction of the thousands of all classes who frequent
it. Not one in a thousand probably perpetrates any
intentional damage to fish, fowl, or flowers.

As the river above all things is, and ought to be, a
place of recreation, care must be particularly taken
that in restraining these practices the enjoyment of
the many be not interfered with. The rational pleasure
of 999 people ought not to be checked because the last
of the thousand acts as a blackguard. This point, too,
bears upon the question of steam-launches. A launch
can pass as softly and quietly as a skiff floating with
the stream. And there is a good deal to be said on
the other side, for the puntsmen stick themselves very
often in the way of every one else ; and if you analyse
fishing for minnows from a punt you will not find it a
noble sport. A river like the Thames, belonging as it
does—or as it ought—to a city like London, should be
managed from the very broadest standpoint. There
should be pleasure for all, and there certainly is no
real difficulty in arranging matters to that end. The
Thames should be like a great aquarium, in which a
certain balance of life has to be kept up. When aquaria
first came into favour such things as snails and weeds
were excluded as eyesores and injurious. But it was
soon discovered that the despised snails and weeds
were absolutely necessary ; an aquarium could not be
maintained in health without them, and now the most
perfect aquarium is the one in which the natural state
is most completely copied. On the same principle it
is evident that too exclusive preservation must be
injurious to the true interests of the river. Fish

enthusiasts, for instance, desire the extinction of
water-fowl—there is not a single aquatic bird which
they do not accuse of damage to fry, spawn, or full-
grown fish ; no, not one, from the heron down to the
tiny grebe. They are nearly as bitter against animals ;
the poor water-vole (or water-rat) even is denounced
and shot. Any one who chooses may watch the water-
rat feeding on aquatic vegetation ; never mind, shoot
him because he's there. There is no other reason.
Bitterest, harshest, most envenomed of all is the
outcry and hunt directed against the otter. It is as
if the otter were a wolf—as if he were as injurious as
the mighty boar whom Meleager and his companions
chased in the days of dim antiquity. What, then,
has the otter done ? Has he ravaged the fields ? does
he threaten the homesteads ? is he at Temple Bar ?
are we to run, as the old song says, from the Dragon ?
The fact is, the ravages attributed to the otter are of
a local character. They are chiefly committed in
those places where fish are more or less confined. If
you keep sheep close together in a pen the wolf who
leaps the hurdles can kill the flock if he chooses.
In narrow waters, and where fish are maintained in
quantities out of proportion to extent, an otter can
work doleful woe. That is to say, those who want too
many fish are those who give the otter his opportunity.

In a great river like the Thames a few otters cannot
do much or lasting injury except in particular places.
The truth, is, that the otter is an ornament to the
river, and more worthy of preservation than any other
creature. He is the last and largest of the wild
creatures who once roamed so freely in the forests

which enclosed Londinium, that fort in the woods
and marshes—marshes which to this day, though
drained and built over, enwrap the nineteenth century
city in thick mists. The red deer are gone, the boar
is gone, the wolf necessarily destroyed—the red deer
can never again drink at the Thames in the dusk
of the evening while our civilization endures. The
otter alone remains—the wildest, the most thoroughly
self-supporting of all living things left—a living link
going back to the days of Cassivelaunus. London
ought to take the greatest interest in the otters of its
river. The shameless way in which every otter that
dares to show itself is shot, trapped, beaten to death,
and literally battered out of existence, should rouse
the indignation of every sportsman and every lover
of nature. The late Rev. John Russell, who, it will
be admitted, was a true sportsman, walked three
thousand miles to see an otter. That was a different
spirit, was it not?

That is the spirit in which the otter in the Thames
should be regarded. Those who offer money rewards
for killing Thames otters ought to be looked on as
those who would offer rewards for poisoning foxes in
Leicestershire. I suppose we shall not see the ospreys
again; but I should like to. Again, on the other side
of the boundary, in the tidal waters, the same sort of
ravenous destruction is carried on against everything
that ventures up. A short time ago a porpoise
came up to Mortlake; now, just think, a porpoise up
from the great sea—that sea to which Londoners
rush with such joy—past Gravesend, past Green-
wich, past the Tower, under London Bridge, past

Westminster and the Houses of Parliament, right up to Mortlake. It is really a wonderful thing that a denizen of the sea, so large and interesting as a porpoise, should come right through the vast City of London. In an aquarium, people would go to see it and admire it, and take their children to see it. What happened? Some one hastened out in a boat, armed with a gun or a rifle, and occupied himself with shooting at it. He did not succeed in killing it, but it was wounded. Some difference here to the spirit of John Russell. If I may be permitted to express an opinion, I think that there is not a single creature, from the sand-marten and the black-headed bunting to the broad-winged heron, from the water-vole to the otter, from the minnow on one side of the tidal boundary to the porpoise on the other—big and little, beasts and birds (of prey or not)—that should not be encouraged and protected on this beautiful river, morally the property of the greatest city in the world.

II.

I looked forward to living by the river with delight, anticipating the long rows I should have past the green eyots and the old houses red-tiled among the trees. I should pause below the weir and listen to the pleasant roar, and watch the fisherman cast again and again with the " transcendent patience " of genius by which alone the Thames trout is captured. Twisting the end of a willow bough round my wrist I could moor myself and rest at ease, though the current roared under the skiff, fresh from the waterfall. A thousand thousand bubbles rising to the surface would whiten the stream—a thousand thousand succeeded by another thousand thousand—and still flowing, no multiple could express the endless number. That which flows continuously by some sympathy is acceptable to the mind, as if thereby it realised its own existence without an end. Swallows would skim the water to and fro as yachts tack, the sandpiper would run along the strand, a black-headed bunting would perch upon the willow; perhaps, as the man of genius fishing and myself made no noise, a kingfisher might come, and we might see him take his prey.

Or I might quit hold of the osier and, entering a shallow backwater, disturb shoals of roach playing where the water was transparent to the bottom, after their wont. Winding in and out like an Indian in his canoe, perhaps traces of an otter might be found—his kitchen mödding—and in the sedges moorhens and wildfowl would hide from me. From its banks I should gather many a flower and notice many a plant, there would be, too, the beautiful water-lily. Or I should row on up the great stream by meadows full of golden buttercups, past fields crimson with trifolium or green with young wheat. Handsome sailing craft would come down spanking before the breeze, laden with bright girls—laughter on board, and love the golden fleece of their argosy.

I should converse with the ancient men of the ferries, and listen to their river lore; they would show me the mark to which the stream rose in the famous year of floods. On again to the cool hostelry whose sign was reflected in the water, where there would be a draught of fine ale for the heated and thirsty sculler.   On again till steeple or tower rising over the trees marked my journey's end for the day, some old town where, after rest and refreshment, there would be a ruin or a timbered house to look at, where I should meet folk full of former days and quaint tales of yore.   Thus to journey on from place to place would be the great charm of the river— travelling by water, not merely sculling to and fro, but really travelling.   Upon a lake I could but row across and back again, and however lovely the scenery might be, still it would always be the same.   But the Thames, upon the river I could really travel, day after day, from Teddington Lock upwards to Windsor, to Oxford, on to quiet Lechlade, or even farther deep into the meadows by Cricklade.   Every hour there would be something interesting, all the freshwater life to study, the very barges would amuse me, and at last there would be the delicious ease of floating home carried by the stream, repassing all that had pleased before.

The time came.   I lived by the river, not far from its widest reaches, before the stream meets its tide. I went down to the eyot for a boat, and my difficulties began.   The crowd of boats lashed to each other in strings ready for the hirer disconcerted me.   There were so many I could not choose; the whole together looked like a broad raft.   Others were hauled on the shore.   Over on the eyot, a little island, there were more boats, boats launched, boats being launched, boats being carried by gentlemen in coloured flannels as carefully as mothers handle their youngest infants,

boats covered in canvas mummy-cases, and dim boats
under roofs, their sharp prows projecting like croco-
diles' snouts. Tricksy outriggers, ready to upset on
narrow keel, were held firmly for the sculler to step
daintily into his place. A strong eight shot by up
the stream, the men all. pulling together as if they
had been one animal. A strong sculler shot by down
the stream, his giant arms bare and the muscles
visible as they rose, knotting and unknotting with the
stroke. Every one on the bank and eyot stopped to
watch him—they knew him, he was training. How
could an amateur venture out and make an exhibition
of himself after such splendid rowing! Still it was
noticeable that plenty of amateurs did venture out,
till the waterway was almost concealed—boated over
instead of bridged—and how they managed to escape
locking their oars together, I could not understand.

I looked again at the boats. Some were outriggers.
I could not get into an outrigger after seeing the great
sculler. The rest were one and all after the same
pattern, *i.e.* with the stern cushioned and prepared
for a lady. Some were larger, and could carry three
or four ladies, but they were all intended for the same
purpose. If the sculler went out in such a boat by
himself he must either sit too forward and so depress
the stem and dig himself, as it were, into the water
at each stroke, or he must sit too much to the rear
and depress the stern, and row with the stem lifted
up, sniffing the air. The whole crowd of boats on hire
were exactly the same; in short, they were built for
woman and not for man, for lovely woman to recline,
parasol in one hand and tiller ropes in the other,

while man—inferior man—pulled and pulled and
pulled as an ox yoked to the plough. They could
only be balanced by man and woman, that was the
only way they could be trimmed on an even keel;
they were like scales, in which the weight on one side
must be counterpoised by a weight in the other.
They were dead against bachelors. They belonged to
woman, and she was absolute mistress of the river.

As I looked, the boats ground together a little,
chafing, laughing at me, making game of me, asking
distinctly what business a man had there without at
least one companion in petticoats? My courage ebbed,
and it was in a feeble voice that I inquired whether
there was no such thing as a little skiff a fellow might
paddle about in? No, nothing of the kind; would a
canoe do? Somehow a canoe would not do. I never
took kindly to canoes, excepting always the Canadian
birch-bark pattern; evidently there was no boat for
me. There was no place on the great river for an
indolent, dreamy particle like myself, apt to drift up
into nooks, and to spend much time absorbing those
pleasures which enter by the exquisite sensitiveness
of the eye—colour, and shade, and form, and the
cadence of glittering ripple and moving leaf. You
must be prepared to pull and push, and struggle for
your existence on the river, as in the vast city hard
by men push and crush for money. You must assert
yourself, and insist upon having your share of the
waterway; you must be perfectly convinced that
yours is the very best style of rowing to be seen;
every one ought to get out of your way. You must
consult your own convenience only, and drive right

into other people's boats, forcing them up into the willows, or against the islands. Never slip along the shore, or into quiet backwaters; always select the more frequented parts, not because you want to go there, but to make your presence known, and go amongst the crowd; and if a few sculls get broken, it only proves how very inferior and how very clumsy other people are. If you see another boat coming down stream in the centre of the river with a broad space on either side for others to pass, at once head your own boat straight at her, and take possession of the way. Or, better still, never look ahead, but pull straight on, and let things happen as they may. Annoy everybody, and you are sure to be right, and to be respected; splash the ladies as you pass with a dexterous flip of the scull, and soak their summer costumes; it is capital sport, and they look so sulky—or is it contemptuous?

There was no such thing as a skiff in which one could quietly paddle about, or gently make way—mile after mile—up the beautiful stream. The boating throng grew thicker, and my courage less and less, till I desperately resorted to the ferry—at all events, I could be rowed over in the ferry-boat, that would be something; I should be on the water, after a fashion —and the ferryman would know a good deal. The burly ferryman cared nothing at all about the river, and merely answered "Yes," or "No;" he was full of the Derby and Sandown; didn't know about the fishing; supposed there were fish; didn't see 'em, nor eat 'em; want a punt? No. So he landed me, desolate and hopeless, on the opposite bank, and I began to understand how the souls felt after Charon

had got them over. They could not have been more
unhappy than I was on the towing-path, as the ferry-
boat receded and left me watching the continuous
succession of boats passing up and down the river.

By-and-by an immense black hulk came drifting
round the bend—an empty barge—almost broadside
across the stream, for the current at the curve
naturally carried it out from the shore. This huge
helpless monster occupied the whole river, and had
no idea where it was going, for it had no fins or
sweeps to guide its course, and the rudder could only
induce it to submit itself lengthways to the stream
after the lapse of some time. The fairway of the
river was entirely taken up by this irresponsible
Frankenstein of the Thames, which some one had
started, but which now did as it liked. Some of the
small craft got up into the willows and waited; some
seemed to narrowly escape being crushed against a
wall on the opposite bank. The bright white sails
of a yacht shook and quivered as its steersman tried
all he knew to coax his vessel an inch more into the
wind out of the monster's path. In vain! He had
to drop down the stream, and lose what it had taken
him half an hour's skill to gain. What a pleasing
monster to meet in the narrow arches of a bridge!
The man in charge leaned on the tiller, and placidly
gazed at the wild efforts of some unskilful oarsmen
to escape collision. In fact, the monster had charge
of the man, and did as it liked with him.

Down the river they drifted together, Frankenstein
swinging round and thrusting his blunt nose first
this way and then that; down the river, blocking

up the narrow passage by the eyot; stopping the
traffic at the lock; out at last into the tidal stream,
there to begin a fresh life of annoyance, and finally
to endanger the good speed of many a fine three-
master and ocean steamer off the docks. The Thames
barge knows no law. No judge, no jury, no Palace
of Justice, no Chancery, no appeal to the Lords has
any terror for the monster barge. It drifts by the
Houses of Parliament with no more respect than it
shows for the lodge of the lock-keeper. It drifts by
Royal Windsor, and cares not. The guns of the
Tower are of no account. There is nothing in the
world so utterly free as this monster.

Often have I asked myself if the bargee at the
tiller, now sucking at his short black pipe, now
munching onions and cheese (the little onions he
pitches on the lawns by the river side, there to take
root and flourish)—if this amiable man has any
notion of his own incomparable position. Just some
inkling of the irony of the situation must, I fancy,
now and then dimly dawn within his grimy brow.
To see all these gentlemen shoved on one side; to be
lying in the way of a splendid Australian clipper;
to stop an incoming vessel, impatient for her berth;
to swing, and sway, and roll as he goes; to bump
the big ships, and force the little ones aside; to slip,
and slide, and glide with the tide, ripples dancing
under the prow, and be master of the world-famed
Thames from source to mouth, is not this a joy for
ever? Liberty is beyond price; now no one is really
free unless he can crush his neighbour's interest
underfoot, like a horse-roller going over a daisy.

Bargee is free, and the ashes of his pipe are worth a king's ransom.

Imagine a great van loaded at the East-end of London with the heaviest merchandise, with bags of iron nails, shot, leaden sheets in rolls, and pig iron; imagine four strong horses—dray-horses—harnessed thereto. Then let the waggoner mount behind in a seat comfortably contrived for him facing the rear, and settle himself down happily among his sacks, light his pipe, and fold his hands untroubled with any worry of reins. Away they go through the crowded city, by the Bank of England, and across into Cheapside, cabs darting this way, carriages that, omnibuses forced up into side-streets, foot traffic suspended till the monster has passed; up Fleet-street, clearing the road in front of them—right through the stream of lawyers always rushing to and fro the Temple and the New Law Courts, along the Strand, and finally in triumph into Rotten Row at five o'clock on a June afternoon. See how they scatter! see how they run! The Row is swept clear from end to end—beauty, fashion, rank,—what are such trifles of an hour? The monster vans grind them all to powder. What such a waggoner might do on land, bargee does on the river.

Of olden time the silver Thames was the chosen mode of travel of Royalty—the highest in the land were rowed from palace to city, or city to palace, between its sunlit banks. Noblemen had their special oarsmen, and were in like manner conveyed, and could any other mode of journeying be equally pleasant? The coal-barge has bumped them all out of the way.

No man dares send forth the commonest cart unless in proper charge, and if the horse is not under control a fine is promptly administered. The coal-barge rolls and turns and drifts as chance and the varying current please. How huge must be the rent in the meshes of the law to let so large a fish go through! But in truth there is no law about it, and to this day no man can confidently affirm that he knows to whom the river belongs. These curious anomalies are part and parcel of our political system, and as I watched the black monster slowly go by with the stream it occurred to me that grimy bargee, with his short pipe and his onions, was really the guardian of the British Constitution.

Hardly had he gone past than a loud Pant! pant! pant! began some way down the river; it came from a tug, whose short puffs of steam produced a giant echo against the walls and quays and houses on the bank. These angry pants sounded high above the splash of oars and laughter, and the chorus of singers in a boat; they conquered all other sounds and noises, and domineered the place. It was impossible to shut the ears to them, or to persuade the mind not to heed. The swallows dipped their breasts; how gracefully they drank on the wing! Pant! pant! pant! The sunlight gleamed on the wake of a four-oar. Pant! pant! pant! The soft wind blew among the trees and over the hawthorn hedge. Pant! pant! pant! Neither the eye nor ear could attend to aught but this hideous uproar. The tug was weak, the stream strong, the barges behind heavy, broad, and deeply laden, so that each puff

and pant and turn of the screw barely advanced the
mass a foot. There are many feet in a mile, and
for all that weary time—Pant! pant! pant! This
dreadful uproar, like that which Don Quixote and
Sancho Panza heard proceeding from the fulling
mill, must be endured. Could not philosophy by
stoic firmness shut out the sound? Can philosophy
shut out anything that is real? A long black streak
of smoke hung over the water, fouling the gleaming
surface. A noise of Dante—hideous, uncompromising
as the rusty hinge of the gate which forbids hope.
Pant! pant! pant!

Once upon a time a Queen of England was rowed
adown the silver Thames to the sweet low sound of
the flute.

At last the noise grew fainter in the distance,
and the black hulls disappeared round the bend.
I walked on up the towing-path. Accidentally lifting
my hand to shade my eyes, I was hailed by a ferryman on the watch. He conveyed me over without
much volition on my part, and set me ashore by the
inn of my imagination. The rooms almost overhung
the water: so far my vision was fulfilled. Within
there was an odour of spirits and spilled ale, a rustle
of sporting papers, talk of racings, and the click of
billiard-balls. Without there were two or three
loafers, half boatmen, half vagabonds, waiting to pick
up stray sixpences—a sort of leprosy of rascal and
sneak in their faces and the lounge of their bodies.
These Thames-side "beach-combers" are a sorry lot,
a special Pariah class of themselves. Some of them
have been men once: perhaps one retains his sculling

skill, and is occasionally engaged by a gentleman to
give him lessons. They regarded me eagerly—they
"spotted" a Thames freshman who might be made
to yield silver; but I walked away down the road
into the village. The spire of the church interested
me, being of shingles—*i.e.* of wooden slates—as the
houses are roofed in America, as houses were roofed
in Elizabethan England; for Young America repro-
duces Old England even in roofs. Some of the
houses so closely approached the churchyard that
the pantry windows on a level with the ground were
partly blocked up by the green mounds of graves.
Borage grew thickly all over the yard, dropping its
blue flowers on the dead. The sharp note of a bugle
rang in the air: they were changing guard, I suppose,
in Wolsey's Palace.

III.

In time I did discover a skiff moored in a little-
visited creek, which the boatman got out for me.
The sculls were rough and shapeless—it is a remarkable fact that sculls always are, unless you have them
made and keep them for your own use. I paddled
up the river; I paused by an osier-grown islet; I
slipped past the barges, and avoided an unskilful
party; it was the morning, and none of the uproarious
as yet were about. Certainly, it was very pleasant.
The sunshine gleamed on the water, broad shadows
of trees fell across; swans floated in the by-channels.
A peacefulness which peculiarly belongs to water
hovered above the river. A house-boat was moored
near the willow-grown shore, and it was evidently

inhabited, for there was a fire smouldering on the
bank, and some linen that had been washed spread
on the bushes to bleach. All the windows of this
gipsy-van of the river were wide open, and the air
and light entered freely into every part of the dwelling-
house under which flowed the stream. A lady was
dressing herself before one of these open windows,
twining up large braids of dark hair, her large arms
bare to the shoulder, and somewhat farther. I
immediately steered out into the channel to avoid
intrusion; but I felt that she was regarding me
with all a matron's contempt for an unknown man
—a mere member of the opposite sex, not introduced,
or of her "set." I was merely a man—no more
than a horse on the bank,—and had she been in her
smock she would have been just as indifferent.

Certainly it was a lovely morning; the old red
palace of the Cardinal seemed to slumber amid its
trees, as if the passage of the centuries had stroked and
soothed it into indolent peace. The meadows rested;
even the swallows, the restless swallows, glided in an
effortless way through the busy air. I could see this,
and yet I did not quite enjoy it; something drew me
away from perfect contentment, and gradually it
dawned upon me that it was the current causing an
unsuspected amount of labour in sculling. The force-
less particles of water, so yielding to the touch, which
slipped aside at the motion of the oar, in their countless myriads ceaselessly flowing grew to be almost a
solid obstruction to the boat. I had not noticed it
for a mile or so; now the pressure of the stream was
becoming evident. I persuaded myself that it was

nothing. I held on by the boathook to a root and
rested, and so went on again. Another mile or
more ; another rest : decidedly sculling against a
swift current is work—downright work. You have
no energy to spare over and above that needed for
the labour of rowing, not enough even to look round
and admire the green loveliness of the shore. I began
to think that I should not get as far as Oxford after
all.

By-and-by, I began to question if rowing on a
river is as pleasant as rowing on a lake, where
you can rest on your oars without losing ground,
where no current opposes progress, and after the
stroke the boat slips ahead some distance of its own
impetus. On the river the boat only travels as
far as you actually pull it at each stroke ; there
is no life in it after the scull is lifted, the impetus dies,
and the craft first pauses and then drifts backward.
I crept along the shore, so near that one scull occasionally grounded, to avoid the main force of the water,
which is in the middle of the river. I slipped behind
eyots and tried all I knew. In vain, the river was
stronger than I, and my arms could not for many
hours contend with the Thames. So faded another
part of my dream. The idea of rowing from one
town to another—of expeditions and travelling across
the country, so pleasant to think of—in practice
became impossible. An athlete bent on nothing but
athleticism—a canoeist thinking of nothing but his
canoe—could accomplish it, setting himself daily so
much work to do, and resolutely performing it. A
dreamer, who wanted to enjoy his passing moment,

and not to keep regular time with his strokes, who wanted to gather flowers, and indulge his luxurious eyes with effects of light and shadow and colour, could not succeed.   The river is for the man of might.

With a weary back at last I gave up the struggle at the foot of a weir, almost in the splash of the cascade.   My best friend, the boathook, kept me stationary without effort, and in time rest restored the strained muscles to physical equanimity.   The roar of the river falling over the dam soothed the mind—the sense of an immense power at hand, working with all its might while you are at ease, has a strangely soothing influence.   It makes me sleepy to see the vast beam of an engine regularly rise and fall in ponderous irresistible labour.   Now at last some fragment of my fancy was realised—a myriad myriad rushing bubbles whitening the stream burst, and were instantly succeeded by myriads more; the boat faintly vibrated as the wild waters shot beneath it; the green cascade, smooth at its first curve, dashed itself into the depth beneath, broken to a million million particles; the eddies whirled, and sucked, and sent tiny whirlpools rotating along the surface; the roar rose or lessened in intensity as the velocity of the wind varied; sunlight sparkled— the warmth inclined the senses to a drowsy idleness. Yonder was the trout fisherman, just as I had imagined him, casting and casting again with that transcendental patience which is genius; his line and the top of his rod formed momentary curves pleasant to look at.   The kingfisher did not come— no doubt he had been shot—but a reed-sparrow did,

in velvet black cap and dainty brown, pottering about
the willow near me. This was really like the beautiful river I had dreamed of. If only we could persuade
ourselves to remain quiescent when we are happy!
If only we would remain still in the armchair as the
last curl of vapour rises from a cigar that has been
enjoyed! If only we would sit still in the shadow
and not go indoors to write that letter! Let happiness alone. Stir not an inch; speak not a word:
happiness is a coy maiden—hold her hand and be
still.

In an evil moment I spied the corner of a newspaper projecting from the pocket of my coat in the
stern-sheets. Folly led me to open that newspaper,
and in it I saw and read a ghastly paragraph. Two
ladies and a gentleman while boating had been carried
by the current against the piles of a weir. The
boat upset; the ladies were rescued, but the unfortunate gentleman was borne over the fall and drowned.
His body had not been recovered; men were watching
the pool day and night till some chance eddy should
bring it to the surface. So perished my dream, and
the coy-maiden happiness left me because I could
not be content to be silent and still. The accident
had not happened at this weir, but it made no difference; I could see all as plainly. A white face, blurred
and indistinct, seemed to rise up from beneath the
rushing bubbles till, just as it was about to jump to
the surface, as things do that come up, down it was
drawn again by that terrible underpull which has
been fatal to so many good swimmers.

Who can keep afloat with a force underneath drag-

ging at the feet? Who can swim when the water—all
bubbles, that is air—gives no resistance to the hands?
Hands and feet slip through the bubbles. You might
as well spring from the parapet of a house and think
to float by striking out as to swim in such a medium.
Sinking under, a hundred tons of water drive the
body to the bottom; there it rotates, it rises, it is
forced down again, a hundred tons of water beat
upon it; the foot, perhaps, catches among stones or
woodwork, and what was once a living being is
imprisoned in death. Enough of this. I unloosed
the boathook, and drifted down with the stream,
anxious to get away from the horrible weir.

These accidents, which are entirely preventible,
happen year after year with lamentable monotony.
Each weir is a little Niagara, and a boat once within
its influence is certain to be driven to destruction.
The current carries it against the piles, where it is
either broken or upset, the natural and reasonable
alarm of the occupants increasing the risk. In
descending the river every boat must approach the
weir, and must pass within a few yards of the
dangerous current. If there is a press of boats one
is often forced out of the proper course into the rapid
part of the stream without any negligence on the part
of those in it. There is nothing to prevent this—
no fence, or boom; no mark, even, between what is
dangerous and what is not; no division whatever.
Persons ignorant of the river may just as likely as
not row right into danger. A vague caution on a
notice-board may or may not be seen; in either case
it gives no directions, and is certainly no protection.

Let the matter be argued from whatever point of view, the fact remains that these accidents occur from the want of an efficient division between the dangerous and the safe part of the approach to a weir. A boom or some kind of fence is required, and how extraordinary it seems that nothing of the kind is done! It is not done because there is no authority, no control, no one responsible. Two or three gentlemen acquainted with aquatics could manage the river from end to end, to the safety and satisfaction of all, if they were entrusted with discretionary powers. Stiff rules and rigid control are not needed; what is wanted is a rational power freely using its discretion. I do not mean a Board with its attendant follies; I mean a small committee, unfettered, untrammelled by "legal advisers" and so forth, merely using their own good sense.

I drifted away from the weir—now grown hideous —and out of hearing of its wailing dirge for the unfortunate. I drifted past more barges coming up, and more steam-tugs; past river lawns, where gay parties were now sipping claret-cup or playing tennis. By-and-by, I began to meet pleasure-boats and to admire their manner of progress. First there came a gentleman in white flannels, walking on the tow-path, with a rope round his waist, towing a boat in which two ladies were comfortably seated. In a while came two more gentlemen in striped flannels, one streaked with gold the other with scarlet, striding side by side and towing a boat in which sat one lady. They were very earnestly at work, pacing in step, their bodies slightly leaning forwards, and every now and then they mopped their faces with handkerchiefs which they carried in their girdles. Something in their slightly-bowed attitude reminded me of the captives depicted on Egyptian monuments, with cords about their necks. How curious is that instinct which makes each sex, in different ways, the willing slave of the other! These human steam-tugs paced and pulled, and drew the varnished craft swiftly against the stream, evidently determined to do a certain distance by a certain hour. As I drifted by without labour, I admired them very much. An interval, and still more gentlemen in flannel, labouring like galley-slaves at the tow-rope, hot, perspiring, and happy after their kind, and ladies under parasols, comfortably seated, cool, and happy after their kind.

Considering upon these things, I began to discern the true and only manner in which the modern Thames is to be enjoyed. Above all things—nothing heroic. Don't scull—don't row—don't haul at tow-ropes—don't swim—don't flourish a fishing-rod. Set your mind at ease. Make friends with two or more athletes, thorough good fellows, good-natured, delighting in their thews and sinews. Explain to them that somehow, don't you see, nature did not bless you with such superabundant muscularity, although there is nothing under the sun you admire so much. Forthwith these good fellows will pet you, and your Thames fortune is made. You take your place in the stern-sheets, happily protected on either side by feminine human nature, and the parasols meeting above shield you from the sun. The tow-rope is adjusted, and the tugs start. The gliding motion

soothes the soul. Feminine boating nature has no
antipathy to the cigarette. A delicious odour, soft as
new-mown hay, a hint of spices and distant flowers
—sunshine dried and preserved, sunshine you can
handle—rises from the smouldering fibres. This is
smoking summer itself. Yonder in the fore part of
the craft I espy certain vessels of glass on which
is the label of Epernay. And of such is peace.

Drifting ever downwards, I approached the creek
where my skiff had to be left; but before I reached
it a "beach-comber," with a coil of cord over his
shoulder, asked me if he should tow me "up to
'Ampton." I shook my head, whereupon he abused
me in such choice terms that I listened abashed at
my ignorance. It had never occurred to me that
swearing could be done like that. It is true we have
been swearing now, generation after generation, these
eight thousand years for certain, and language
expands with use. It is also true that we are all
educated now. Shakespeare is credited with knowing
everything, past or future, but I doubt if he knew how
a Thames "beach-comber" can curse in these days.

The Thames is swearing free. You must moderate
your curses on the Queen's highway; you must not
be even profane in the streets, lest you be taken
before the magistrates; but on the Thames you may
swear as the wind blows—howsoever you list. You
may begin at the mouth, off the Nore, and curse your
way up to Cricklade. A hundred miles for swearing
is a fine preserve. It is one of the marvels of our
civilization.

Aided by scarce a touch of the sculls the stream

drifted me up into the creek, and the boatman took
charge of his skiff. "Shall I keep her handy for
you, sir?" he said, thinking to get me down every
day as a newcomer. I begged him not to put himself
to any trouble, still he repeated that he would keep
her ready. But in the road I shook off the dust of
my feet against the river, and earnestly resolved
never, never again to have anything to do with it (in
the heroic way) lower down than Henley.

THE SINGLE-BARREL GUN.

THE single-barrel gun has passed out of modern sport;
but I remember mine with regret, and think I shall
some day buy another. I still find that the best
double-barrel seems top-heavy in comparison; in
poising it the barrels have a tendency to droop.
Guns, of course, are built to balance and lie level in
the hand, so as to almost aim themselves as they
come to the shoulder; and those who have always
shot with a double-barrel are probably quite satisfied
with the gun on that score. To me there seems too
much weight in the left hand and towards the end of
the gun. Quickness of firing keeps the double-barrel
to the front; but suppose a repeater were to be
invented, some day, capable of discharging two
cartridges in immediate succession? And if two
cartridges, why not three? An easy thought, but a
very difficult one to realise. Something in the *power*
of the double-barrel—the overwhelming odds it affords
the sportsman over bird and animal—pleases. A
man feels master of the copse with a double-barrel;
and such a sense of power, though only over feeble
creatures, is fascinating. Besides, there is the delight
of effect; for a clever right and left is sure of applause,

and makes the gunner feel "good" in himself. Doubtless, if three barrels could be managed, three barrels would be more salable than doubles. One gun-maker has a four-barrel gun, quite a light weight too, which would be a tremendous success if the creatures would obligingly run and fly a little slower, so that all four cartridges could be got in. But that they will not do. For the present, the double-barrel is the gun of the time.

Still I mean some day to buy a single-barrel, and wander with it as of old along the hedges, aware that if I am not skilful enough to bring down with the first shot I shall lose my game. It is surprising how confident of that one shot you may get after a while. On the one hand, it is necessary to be extremely keen ; on the other, to be sure of your own self-control, not to fire uselessly. The bramble-bushes on the shore of the ditch ahead might cover a hare. Through the dank and dark-green aftermath a rabbit might suddenly come bounding, disturbed from the furrow where he had been feeding. On the sandy paths which the rabbits have made aslant up the mound, and on their terraces, where they sit and look out from under the boughs, acorns have dropped ripe from the tree. Where there are acorns there may be pheasants ; they may crouch in the fern and dry grey grass of the hedge thinking you do not see them, or else rush through and take wing on the opposite side. The only chance of a shot is as the bird passes a gap—visible while flying a yard—just time to pull the trigger. But I would rather have that chance than have to fire between the bars of a gate ; for the horizontal lines cause an optical illusion, making the object appear in a different position from what it really is in, and half the pellets are sure to be buried in the rails. Wood-pigeons, when eagerly stuffing their crops with acorns, sometimes forget their usual caution; and, walking slowly, I have often got right underneath one—as unconscious of his presence as he was of mine, till a sudden dashing of wings against boughs and leaves announced his departure. This he always makes on the opposite side of the oak, so as to have the screen of the thick branches between himself and the gunner. The wood-pigeon, starting like this from a tree, usually descends in the first part of his flight, a gentle downward curve followed by an upward rise, and thus comes into view at the lower part of the curve. He still seems within shot, and to afford a good mark; and yet experience has taught me that it is generally in vain to fire. His stout quills protect him at the full range of the gun. Besides, a wasted shot alarms everything within several hundred yards; and in stalking with a single-barrel it needs as much knowledge to choose when not to fire as when you may.

The most exciting work with the single-barrel was woodcock shooting; woodcock being by virtue of rarity a sort of royal game, and a miss at a woodcock a terrible disappointment. They have a trick of skimming along the very summit of a hedge, and looking so easy to kill; but, as they fly, the tops of tall briers here, willow-rods next, or an ash-pole often intervene, and the result is apt to be a bough cut off and nothing more. Snipes, on the contrary, I felt sure of with the single-barrel, and never could hit them so well with a double. Either at starting, before the snipe got into his twist, or waiting till he had finished that uncertain movement, the single-barrel seemed to drop the shot with certainty. This was probably because of its perfect natural balance, so that it moved as if on a pivot. With the single I had nothing to manage but my own arms; with the other I was conscious that I had a gun also. With the single I could kill farther, no matter what it was. The single was quicker at short shots—snap-shots, as at rabbits darting across a narrow lane; and surer at long shots, as at a hare put out a good way ahead by the dog.

For everything but the multiplication of slaughter I liked the single best; I had more of the sense of woodcraft with it. When we consider how helpless a partridge is, for instance, before the fierce blow of shot, it does seem fairer that the gunner should have but one chance at the bird. Partridges at least might be kept for single-barrels: great bags of partridges never seemed to me quite right. Somehow it seems to me that to take so much advantage as the double-barrel confers is not altogether in the spirit of sport. The double-barrel gives no "law." At least to those who love the fields, the streams, and woods for their own sake, the single-barrel will fill the bag sufficiently, and will permit them to enjoy something of the zest men knew before the invention of weapons not only of precision but of repetition: inventions that rendered them too absolute masters of the situation. A single-barrel will soon make a sportsman the keenest of shots. The gun itself can be built to an exquisite perfection—lightness, handiness, workmanship, and performance of the very best. It is said that you can change from a single-barrel shot-gun to a sporting rifle and shoot with the rifle almost at once; while many who have been used to the slap-dash double cannot do anything for some time with a rifle. More than one African explorer has found his single-barrel smooth-bore the most useful of all the pieces in his battery; though, of course, of much larger calibre than required in our fields.

THE HAUNT OF THE HARE.

It is never so much winter in the country as it is in the town. The trees are still there, and in and about them birds remain. "Quip! whip!" sounds from the elms; "Whip! quip!" Redwing thrushes threaten with the "whip" those who advance towards them; they spend much of the day in the elm-tops. Thick tussocks of old grass are conspicuous at the skirt of a hedge; half green, half grey, they contrast with the bare thorn. From behind one of these tussocks a hare starts, his black-tipped ears erect, his long hinder limbs throwing him almost like a grasshopper over the sward—no creature looks so handsome or startling, and it is always a pleasant surprise to see him. Pheasant or partridge do not surprise in the least—they are no more than any other bird; but a hare causes quite a different feeling. He is perfectly wild, unfed, untended, and then he is the largest animal to be shot in the fields. A rabbit slips along the mound, under bushes and behind stoles, but a hare bolts for the open, and hopes in his speed. He leaves the straining spaniel behind, and the distance between them increases as they go. The spaniel's broad hind paws are thrown wide apart as he runs, striking outwards as well as backwards,

and his large ears are lifted by the wind of his
progress. Overtaken by the cartridge, still the hare,
as he lies in the dewy grass, is handsome; lift him
up and his fur is full of colour, there are layers of
tint, shadings of brown within it, one under the other,
and the surface is exquisitely clean. The colours are
not really bright, at least not separately; but they
are so clean and so clear that they give an impression
of warmth and brightness. Even in the excitement
of sport regret cannot but be felt at the sight of those
few drops of blood about the mouth which indicate
that all this beautiful workmanship must now cease
to be. Had he escaped the sportsman would not
have been displeased.

The black bud-sheaths of the ash may furnish a comparison for his ear-tips; the brown brake in October
might give one hue for his fur; the yellow or buff
bryony leaf perhaps another; the clematis is not whiter
than the white part. His colours, as those of so many
of our native wild creatures, appear selected from the
woods, as if they had been gathered and skilfully
mingled together. They can be traced or paralleled
in the trees, the bushes, grasses, or flowers, as if extracted from them by a secret alchemy. In the
plumage of the partridge there are tints that may be
compared with the brown corn, the brown ripe grains
rubbed from the ear; it is in the corn-fields that
the partridge delights. There the young brood are
sheltered, there they feed and grow plump. The red
tips of other feathers are reflections of the red sorrel
of the meadows. The grey fur of the rabbit resembles
the grey ash hue of the underwood in which he hides.

A common plant in moist places, the figwort, bears small velvety flowers, much the colour of the red velvet topknot of the goldfinch, the yellow on whose wings is like the yellow bloom of the furze which he frequents in the winter, perching cleverly on its prickly extremities. In the woods, in the bark of the trees, the varied shades of the branches as their size diminishes, the adhering lichens, the stems of the underwood, now grey, now green; the dry stalks of plants, brown, white, or dark, all the innumerable minor hues that cross and interlace, there is suggested the woven texture of tints found on the wings of birds. For brighter tones the autumn leaves can be resorted to, and in summer the finches rising from the grass spring upwards from among flowers that could supply them with all their colours. But it is not so much the brighter as the undertones that seem to have been drawn from the woodlands or fields. Although no such influence has really been exerted by the trees and plants upon the living creatures, yet it is pleasant to trace the analogy. Those who would convert it into a scientific fact are met with a dilemma to which they are usually oblivious, *i.e.* that most birds migrate, and the very tints which in this country might perhaps, by a stretch of argument, be supposed to conceal them, in a distant climate with a different foliage, or none, would render them conspicuous. Yet it is these analogies and imaginative comparisons which make the country so delightful.

One day in autumn, after toiling with their guns, which are heavy in the September heats, across the

fields and over the hills, the hospitable owner of the
place suddenly asked his weary and thirsty friend
which he would have, champagne, ale, or spirits.
They were just then in the midst of a cover, the trees
kept off the wind, the afternoon sun was warm, and
thirst very natural. They had not been shooting in
the cover, but had to pass through to other corn-
fields. It seemed a sorry jest to ask which would be
preferred in that lonely and deserted spot, miles
from home or any house whence refreshment could
be obtained—wine, spirits, or ale ?—an absurd question, and irritating under the circumstances. As it was
repeated persistently, however, the reply was at length
given, in no very good humour, and wine chosen.
Forthwith putting down his gun, the interrogator
pushed in among the underwood, and from a cavity
concealed beneath some bushes drew forth a bottle of
champagne. He had several of these stores hidden
in various parts of the domain, ready whichever way
the chance of sport should direct their footsteps.

Now the dry wild parsnip, or "gicks," five feet
high, stands dead and dry, its jointed tube of dark
stem surmounted with circular frills or umbels ; the
teazle heads are brown, the great burdocks leafless,
and their burs, still adhering, are withered ; the
ground, almost free of obstruction, is comparatively
easy to search over, but the old sportsman is too
cunning to bury his wine twice in the same place,
and it is no use to look about. No birds in last
year's nests—the winds have torn and upset the
mossy structures in the bushes ; no champagne in
last year's cover. The driest place is under the firs,

where the needles have fallen and strew the surface thickly. Outside the wood, in the waggon-track, the beech leaves lie on the side of the mound, dry and shrivelled at the top, but stir them, and under the top layer they still retain the clear brown of autumn.

The ivy trailing on the bank is moist and freshly green. There are two tints of moss; one light, the other deeper—both very pleasant and restful to the eye. These beds of moss are the greenest and brightest of the winter's colours. Besides these there are ale-hoof, or ground-ivy leaves (not the ivy that climbs trees), violet leaves, celandine mars, primrose mars, foxglove mars, teazle mars, and barren strawberry leaves, all green in the midst of winter. One tiny white flower of barren strawberry has ventured to bloom. Round about the lower end of each maple stick, just at the ground, is a green wrap of moss. Though leafless above, it is green at the foot. At the verge of the ploughed field below, exposed as it is, chickweed, groundsel, and shepherd's-purse are flowering. About a little thorn there hang withered red berries of bryony, as if the bare thorn bore fruit; the bine of the climbing plant clings to it still; there are traces of "old man's beard," the white fluffy relics of clematis bloom, stained brown by the weather; green catkins droop thickly on the hazel. Every step presents some item of interest, and thus it is that it is never so much winter in the country. Where fodder has been thrown down in a pasture field for horses, a black congregation of rooks has crowded together in a ring. A solitary pole for trapping hawks stands on the sloping ground outside the cover. These poles are visited every morning when the trap is there, and the captured creature put out of pain. Of the cruelty of the trap itself there can be no doubt; but it is very unjust to assume that therefore those connected with sport are personally cruel. In a farmhouse much frequented by rats, and from which they cannot be driven out, these animals are said to have discovered a means of defying the gin set for them. One such gin was placed in the cheese-room, near a hole from which they issued, but they dragged together pieces of straw, little fragments of wood, and various odds and ends, and so covered the pan that the trap could not spring. They formed, in fact, a bridge over it.

Red and yellow fungi mark decaying places on the trunks and branches of the trees; their colour is brightest when the boughs are bare. By a streamlet wandering into the osier beds the winter gnats dance in the sunshine, round about an old post covered with ivy, on which green berries are thick. The warm sunshine gladdens the hearts of the moorhens floating on the water yonder by the bushes, and their singular note, "coorg-coorg," is uttered at intervals. In the plantation close to the house a fox resides as safe as King Louis in "Quentin Durward," surrounded with his guards and archers and fortified towers, though tokens of his midnight rambles, in the shape of bones, strew the front of his castle. He crosses the lawn in sight of the windows occasionally, as if he really knew and understood that his life is absolutely safe at ordinary times, and that he need beware of nothing but the hounds.

THE BATHING SEASON.

Most people who go on the West Pier at Brighton walk at once straight to the farthest part. This is the order and custom of pier promenading; you are to stalk along the deck till you reach the end, and there go round and round the band in a circle like a horse tethered to an iron pin, or else sit down and admire those who do go round and round. No one looks back at the gradually extending beach and the fine curve of the shore. No one lingers where the surf breaks—immediately above it—listening to the remorseful sigh of the dying wave as it sobs back to the sea. There, looking downwards, the white edge of the surf recedes in hollow crescents, curve after curve for a mile or more, one succeeding before the first can disappear and be replaced by a fresh wave. A faint mistiness hangs above the beach at some distance, formed of the salt particles dashed into the air and suspended. At night, if the tide chances to be up, the white surf rushing in and returning immediately beneath has a strange effect, especially in its pitiless regularity. If one wave seems to break a little higher it is only in appearance, and because you have not watched long enough. In a certain

number of times another will break there again;
presently one will encroach the merest trifle; after
a while another encroaches again, and the apparent
irregularity is really sternly regular. The free wave
has no liberty—it does not act for itself,—no real
generous wildness. "Thus far and no farther," is
not a merciful saying. Cold and dread and pitiless,
the wave claims its due—it stretches its arms to the
fullest length, and does not pause or hearken to the
desire of any human heart. Hopeless to appeal to
is the unseen force that sends the white surge underneath to darken the pebbles to a certain line. The
wetted pebbles are darker than the dry; even in the
dusk they are easily distinguished. Something merci-
less is there not in this conjunction of restriction
and impetus? Something outside human hope and
thought—indifferent—cold?

Considering in this way, I wandered about fifty
yards along the pier, and sat down in an abstracted
way on the seat on the right side. Beneath, the clear
green sea rolled in crestless waves towards the shore
—they were moving "without the animation of the
wind," which had deserted them two days ago, and
a hundred miles out at sea. Slower and slower, with
an indolent undulation, rising and sinking of mere
weight and devoid of impetus, the waves passed on,
scarcely seeming to break the smoothness of the
surface. At a little distance it seemed level; yet
the boats every now and then sank deeply into the
trough, and even a large fishing-smack rolled heavily.
For it is the nature of a groundswell to be exceedingly
deceptive. Sometimes the waves are so far apart

that the sea actually is level—smooth as the surface of a polished dining-table—till presently there appears a darker line slowly approaching, and a wave of considerable size comes in, advancing exactly like the crease in the cloth which the housemaid spreads on the table—the air rolling along underneath it forms a linen imitation of the groundswell. These unexpected rollers are capital at upsetting boats just touching the beach; the boat is broadside on and the occupants in the water in a second. To-day the groundswell was more active, the waves closer together, not having had time to forget the force of the extinct gale. Yet the sea looked calm as a millpond—just the morning for a bath.

Along the yellow line where sand and pebbles meet there stood a gallant band, in gay uniforms, facing the water. Like the imperial legions who were ordered to charge the ocean, and gather the shells as spoils of war, the cohorts gleaming in purple and gold extended their front rank—their fighting line one to a yard—along the strand. Some tall and stately; some tall and slender; some well developed and firm on their limbs; some gentle in attitude, even in their war dress; some defiant; perhaps forty or fifty, perhaps more, ladies; a splendid display of womanhood in the bright sunlight. Blue dresses, pink dresses, purple dresses, trimmings of every colour; a gallant show. The eye had but just time to receive these impressions as it were with a blow of the camera—instantaneous photography—when, boom! the groundswell was on them, and, heavens, what a change! They disappeared. An arm projected here, possibly a foot yonder, tresses floated on the surface like seaweed, but bodily they were gone. The whole rank from end to end was overthrown—more than that, overwhelmed, buried, interred in water like Pharaoh's army in the Red Sea. Crush! It had come on them like a mountain. The wave so clear, so beautifully coloured, so cool and refreshing, had struck their delicate bodies with the force of a ton weight. Crestless and smooth to look at, in reality that treacherous roller weighed at least a ton to a yard.

Down went each fair bather as if hit with shot from a Gatling gun. Down she went, frantically, and vainly grasping at a useless rope; down with water driven into her nostrils, with a fragment, a tiny blade, of seaweed forced into her throat, choking her; crush on the hard pebbles, no feather bed, with the pressure of a ton of water overhead, and the strange rushing roar it makes in the ears. Down she went, and at the same time was dragged head foremost, sideways, anyhow, but dragged—*ground* along on the bitter pebbles some yards higher up the beach, each pebble leaving its own particular bruise, and the suspended sand filling the eyes. Then the wave left her, and she awoke from the watery nightmare to the bright sunlight, and the hissing foam as it subsided, prone at full length, high and dry like a stranded wreck. Perhaps her head had tapped the wheel of the machine in a friendly way—a sort of genial battering ram. The defeat was a perfect rout; yet they recovered position immediately. I fancy I did see one slip limply to cover; but the main body rose manfully, and picked their way with delicate feet on the hard, hard stones back again to the water, again to meet their inevitable fate.

The white ankles of the blonde gleaming in the sunshine were distinguishable, even at that distance, from the flesh tint of the brunette beside her, and these again from the swarthiness of still darker ankles, which did not gleam, but had a subdued colour like dead gold. The foam of a lesser wave ran up and touched their feet submissively. Three young girls in pink clustered together; one crouched with her back to the sea and glanced over her timorous shoulder. Another lesser wave ran up and left a fringe of foam before them. I looked for a moment out to sea and saw the smack roll heavily, the big wave was coming. By now the bathers had gathered confidence, and stepped, a little way at a time, closer and closer down to the water. Some even stood where each lesser wave rose to their knees. Suddenly a few leant forwards, pulling their ropes taut, and others turned sideways; these were the more experienced or observant. Boom! The big roller broke near the pier and then ran along the shore; it did not strike the whole length at once, it came in aslant and rushed sideways. The three in pink went first—they were not far enough from their machine to receive its full force, it barely reached to the waist, and really I think it was worse for them. They were lifted off their feet and shot forward with their heads under water; one appeared to be under the two others, a confused mass of pink. Their white feet emerged behind the roller, and as it sank it drew them back,

grinding them over the pebbles : every one knows how
pebbles grate and grind their teeth as a wave subsides.
Left lying on their faces, I guessed from their attitudes
that they had dug their finger-nails into the pebbles
in an effort to seize something that would hold.
Somehow they got on their knees and crept up the
slope of the beach. Beyond these three some had
been standing about up to their knees; these were
simply buried as before—quite concealed and thrown
like beams of timber, head first, feet first, high up on
shore. Group after group went down as the roller
reached them, and the sea was dyed for a minute with
blue dresses, purple dresses, pink dresses; they
coloured the wave which submerged them. From
end to end the whole rank was again overwhelmed,
nor did any position prove of advantage; those who
sprang up as the wave came were simply turned over
and carried on their backs, those who tried to dive
under were swept back by the tremendous under-rush.
Sitting on the beach, lying at full length, on hands
and knees, lying on this side or that, doubled up—
there they were, as the roller receded, in every dis-
consolate attitude imaginable; the curtain rose and
disclosed the stage in disorder. Again I thought I
saw one or two limp to their machines, but the main
body adjusted themselves and faced the sea.

Was there ever such courage ? National untaught
courage—inbred, and not built of gradual instruction
as it were in hardihood. Yet some people hesitate
to give women the franchise ! actually, a miserable
privilege which any poor fool of a man may exercise.

I was philosophizing admirably in this strain when

first a shadow came and then the substance, that is, a gentleman sat down by me and wished me good morning, in a slightly different accent to that we usually hear. I looked wistfully at the immense length of empty seats; on both sides of the pier for two hundred yards or more there extended an endless empty seat. Why could not he have chosen a spot to himself? Why must he place himself just here, so close as to touch me? Four hundred yards of vacant seats, and he could not find room for himself.

It is a remarkable fact in natural history that one's elbow is sure to be jogged. It does not matter what you do; suppose you paint in the most secluded spot, and insert yourself, moreover, in the most inconspicuous part of that spot, some vacant physiognomy is certain to intrude, glaring at you with glassy eye. Suppose you do nothing (like myself), no matter where you do it some inane humanity obtrudes itself. I took out my note-book once in a great open space at the Tower of London, a sort of court or place of arms, quite open and a gunshot across; there was no one in sight, and if there had been half a regiment they could have passed (and would have passed) without interference. I had scarcely written three lines when the pencil flew up the page, some hulking lout having brushed against me. He could not find room for himself. A hundred yards of width was not room enough for him to go by. He meant no harm; it did not occur to him that he could be otherwise than welcome. He was the sort of man who calmly sleeps on your

shoulder in a train, and merely replaces his head
if you wake him twenty times. The very same thing
has happened to me in the parks, and in country
fields; particularly it happens at the British Museum
and the picture galleries, there is room sufficient in
all conscience; but if you try to make a note or a
rough memorandum sketch you get a jog. There is
a jogger everywhere, just as there is a buzzing fly
everywhere in summer. The jogger travels, too.

One day, while studying in the Louvre, I am certain
three or four hundred French people went by me,
mostly provincials I fancy, country-folk, in short,
from their dress, which was not Parisian, and their
accent, which was not of the Boulevards. Of all
these not one interfered with me; they did not
approach within four or five feet. How grateful I
felt towards them! One man and his sweetheart, a
fine southern girl with dark eyes and sun-browned
cheeks, sat down near me on one of the scanty seats
provided. The man put his umbrella and his hat
on the seat beside him. What could be more natural?
No one else was there, and there was room for three
more couples. Instantly an official—an authority!
—stepped hastily forward from the shadow of some
sculpture (beasts of prey abide in darkness), snatched
up the umbrella and hat, and rudely dashed them
on the floor. In a flow of speech he explained that
nothing must be placed on the seats. The man, who
had his handkerchief in his hand, quietly dropped it
into his hat on the floor and replied nothing. This
was an official "jogger." I felt indignant to see and
hear people treated in this rough manner; but the

provincial was used to the jogger system and heeded it not. My own jogger was coming. Three to four hundred country-folk had gone by gently and in a gentlemanly way. Then came an English gentleman, middle-aged, florid, not much tinctured with art or letters, but garnished with huge gold watchchain and with wealth as it were bulging out of his waistcoat pocket. This gentleman positively walked into me, pushed me—literally pushed me aside and took my place, a place valuable to me at that moment for one special aspect, and having shoved me aside, gazed about him through his eyeglass, I suppose to discover what it was interested me. He was a genuine, thoroughbred jogger. The vast galleries of the Louvre had not room enough for him. He was one of the most successful joggers in the world, I feel sure; any family might be proud of him. While I am thus digressing, the bathers have gone over thrice.

The individual who had sat himself down by me produced a little box and offered me a lozenge. I did not accept it; he took one himself in token that they were harmless. Then he took a second, and a third, and began to tell me of their virtues; they cured this and they alleviated that, they were the greatest discovery of the age; this universal lozenge was health in the waistcoat pocket, a medicine-chest between finger and thumb; the secret had been extracted at last, and nature had given up the ghost as it were of her hidden physic. His eloquence conjured up in my mind a vision of the rocks beside the Hudson river papered over with acres of adver-

tising posters. But no; by his further conversation
I found that I had mentally slandered him; he was
not a proprietor of patent medicine; he was a man
of education and private means; he belonged to a
much higher profession, in fact he was a "jogger"
travelling about from place to place—"globe-trotting"
from capital city to watering-place—all over the
world in the exercise of his function. I had wondered
if his accent was American (petroleum-American),
or German, or Italian, or Russian, or what. Now I
wondered no longer, for the jogger is cosmopolitan.
When he had exhausted his lozenge he told me how
many times the screw of the steamer revolved while
carrying him across the Pacific from Yokohama to
San Francisco. I nearly suggested that it was about
equal to the number of times his tongue had vibrated
in the last ten minutes. The bathers went over twice
more. I was anxious to take note of their bravery,
and turned aside, leaning over the iron back of the
seat. He went on just the same; a hint was no
more to him than a feather bed to an ironclad.

My rigid silence was of no avail; so long as my ears
were open he did not care. He was a very energetic
jogger. However, it occurred to me to try another
plan: I turned towards him (he would much rather
have had my back) and began to talk in the most
strident tones I could command. I pointed out to
him that the pier was decked like a vessel, that the
cliffs were white, that a lady passing had a dark blue
dress on, which did not suit with the green sea, not
because it was blue, but because it was the wrong
tint of blue; I informed him that the Pavilion was

once the residence of royalty, and similar novelties; all in a string without a semicolon. His eyes opened; he fumbled with his lozenge-box, said "Good morning," and went on up the pier. I watched him go— English-Americano-Germano-Franco-Prussian-Russian-Chinese-New Zealander that he was. But he was not a man of genius; you could choke him off by talking. Still he had effectually jogged me and spoiled my contemplative enjoyment of the bathers' courage; upon the whole I thought I would go down on the beach now and see them a little closer. The truth is, I suppose, that it is people like myself who are in the wrong, or are in the way. What business had I to make a note in the Tower yard, or study in the Louvre? what business have I to think, or indulge myself in an idea? What business has any man to paint, or sketch, or do anything of the sort? I suppose the joggers are in the right.

Dawdling down Whitehall one day a jogger nailed me—they come to me like flies to honey—and got me to look at his pamphlet. He went about, he said, all his time distributing them as a duty for the safety of the nation. The pamphlet was printed in the smallest type, and consisted of extracts from various prophetical authors, pointing out the enormity of the Babylonian Woman, or the City of Scarlet, or some such thing; the gist being the bitterest— almost scurrilous—attack on the Church of Rome. The jogger told me, with tears of pride in his eyes and a glorified countenance, that only a few days before, in the waiting-room of a railway station, he had the pleasure to present his pamphlet to Cardinal

Manning. And the Cardinal bowed and put it in his pocket.

Just as everybody walks on the sunny side of Regent-street, so there are certain spots on the beach where people crowd together. This is one of them; just west of the West Pier there is a fair between eleven and one every bright morning. Everybody goes because everybody else does. Mamma goes down to bathe with her daughters and the little ones; they take two machines at least; the pater comes to smoke his cigar; the young fellows of the family-party come to look at "the women," as they irreverently speak of the sex. So the story runs on *ad infinitum,* down to the shoeless ones that turn up everywhere. Every seat is occupied; the boats and small yachts are filled; some of the children pour pebbles into the boats, some carefully throw them out; wooden spades are busy; sometimes they knock each other on the head with them, sometimes they empty pails of sea-water on a sister's frock. There is a squealing, squalling, screaming, shouting, singing, bawling, howling, whistling, tin-trumpeting, and every luxury of noise. Two or three bands work away; niggers clatter their bones; a conjurer in red throws his heels in the air; several harps strum merrily different strains; fruit-sellers push baskets into folks' faces; sellers of wretched needlework and singular baskets coated with shells thrust their rubbish into people's laps. These shell baskets date from George IV. The gingerbeer men and the newsboys cease not from troubling. Such a volume of uproar, such a complete organ of discord— I mean a whole organful—cannot be found anywhere

else on the face of the earth in so comparatively small
a space. It is a sort of triangular plot of beach
crammed with everything that ordinarily annoys the
ears and offends the sight.

Yet you hear nothing and see nothing; it is perfectly comfortable, perfectly jolly and exhilarating, a
preferable spot to any other. A sparkle of sunshine
on the breakers, a dazzling gleam from the white
foam, a warm sweet air, light and brightness and
champagniness; altogether lovely. The way in which
people lie about on the beach, their legs this way, and
their arms that, their hats over their eyes, their utter
give-themselves-up expression of attitude is enough in
itself to make a reasonable being contented. Nobody
cares for anybody; they drowned Mrs. Grundy long
ago. The ancient philosopher (who had a mind to
eat a fig) held that a nail driven into wood could only
support a certain weight. After that weight was
exceeded either the wood must break or the nail
come out. Yonder is a wooden seat put together
with nails—a flimsy contrivance, which defies all
rules of gravity and adhesion. One leg leans one
way, the other in the opposite direction; very lame
legs indeed. Careful folk would warn you not to sit
on it lest it should come to pieces. The music, I
suppose, charms it, for it holds together in the most
marvellous manner. Four people are sitting on it,
four big ones, middle-aged, careful people; every
moment the legs gape wide apart, the structure
visibly stretches and yields and sinks in the pebbles,
yet it does not come down. The stoutest of all sits
actually over the lame legs, reading his paper quite

oblivious of the odd angle his plump person makes, quite unconscious of the threatened crack—crash ! It does not happen. A sort of magnetism sticks it together; it is in the air; it makes things go right that ought to go wrong. Awfully naughty place; no sort of idea of rightness here. Humming and strumming, and singing and smoking, splashing, and sparkling ; a buzz of voices and booming of sea ! If they could only be happy like this always !

Mamma has a tremendous fight over the bathing-dresses, her own, of course ; the bathing woman cannot find them, and denies that she had them, and by-and-by, after half an hour's exploration, finds them all right, and claims commendation for having put them away so safely. Then there is the battle for a machine. The nurse has been keeping guard on the steps, to seize it the instant the occupant comes out. At last they get it, and the wonder is how they pack themselves in it. Boom ! The bathers have gone over again, I know. The rope stretches as the men at the capstan go round, and heave up the machines one by one before the devouring tide.

As it is not at all rude, but the proper thing to do, I thought I would venture a little nearer (not too obtrusively near) and see closer at hand how brave womanhood faced the rollers. There was a young girl lying at full length at the edge of the foam. She reclined parallel to the beach, not with her feet towards the sea, but so that it came to her side. She was clad in some material of a gauzy and yet opaque texture, permitting the full outline and the least movement to be seen. The colour I do not exactly know

how to name; they could tell you at the Magasin du
Louvre, where men understand the hues of garments
as well as women. I presume it was one of the many
tints that are called at large "creamy." It suited
her perfectly. Her complexion was in the faintest
degree swarthy, and yet not in the least like what a
lady would associate with that word. The difficulty
in describing a colour is that different people take
different views of the terms employed; ladies have
one scale founded a good deal on dress, men another,
and painters have a special (and accurate) gamut
which they use in the studio. This was a clear
swarthiness—a translucent swarthiness—clear as the
most delicate white. There was something in the
hue of her neck as freely shown by the loose bathing
dress, of her bare arms and feet, somewhat recalling
to mind the kind of beauty attributed to the Queen
of Egypt. But it was more delicate. Her form was
almost fully developed, more so than usual at her
age. Again and again the foam rushed up deep
enough to cover her limbs, but not sufficiently so to
hide her chest, as she was partly raised on one
arm. Washed thus with the purest whiteness of the
sparkling foam, her beauty gathered increase from
the touch of the sea. She swayed slightly as the
water reached her, she was luxuriously recked to and
fro. The waves toyed with her; they came and
retired, happy in her presence; the breeze and the
sunshine were there.

Standing somewhat back, the machines hid the
waves from me till they reached the shore, so that
I did not observe the heavy roller till it came and

broke. A ton of water fell on her, crush! The edge
of the wave curled and dropped over her, the arch
bowed itself above her, the keystone of the wave fell
in. She was under the surge while it rushed up and
while it rushed back; it carried her up to the steps
of the machine and back again to her original position.
When it subsided she simply shook her head, raised
herself on one arm, and adjusted herself parallel to
the beach as before.

Let any one try this, let any one lie for a few
minutes just where the surge bursts, and he will
understand what it means. Men go out to the length
of their ropes—past and outside the line of the
breakers, or they swim still farther out and ride at
ease where the wave, however large, merely lifts them
pleasantly as it rolls under. But the smashing force
of the wave is where it curls and breaks, and it is
there that the ladies wait for it. It is these breakers
in a gale that tear to pieces and destroy the best-built
ships once they touch the shore, scattering their
timbers as the wind scatters leaves. The courage
and the endurance women must possess to face a
groundswell like this!

All the year they live in luxury and ease, and are
shielded from everything that could hurt. A bruise—
a lady to receive a bruise; it is not to be thought of!
If a ruffian struck a lady in Hyde Park the world
would rise from its armchair in a fury of indignation.
These waves and pebbles bruise them as they list.
They do not even flinch. There must, then, be a
natural power of endurance in them.

It is unnecessary, and yet I was proud to see it. An

English lady could do it; but could any other?—
unless, indeed, an American of English descent. Still,
it is a barbarous thing, for bathing could be easily
rendered pleasant. The cruel roller receded, the soft
breeze blew, the sunshine sparkled, the gleaming
foam rushed up and gently rocked her. The Infanta
Cleopatra lifted her arm gleaming wet with spray,
and extended it indolently; the sun had only given
her a more seductive loveliness. How much more
enjoyable the sea and breeze and sunshine when one
is gazing at something so beautiful. That arm,
rounded and soft——

"Excuse me, sir, but your immortal soul"—a hand
was placed on my elbow. I turned, and saw a beam-
ing face; a young lady, elegantly dressed, placed a
fly-sheet of good intentions in my fingers. The fair
jogger beamed yet more sweetly as I took it, and
went on among the crowd. When I looked back
the Infanta Cleopatra had ascended into her machine.
I had lost the last few moments of loveliness.

UNDER THE ACORNS.

Coming along a woodland lane, a small round and glittering object in the brushwood caught my attention. The ground was but just hidden in that part of the wood with a thin growth of brambles, low, and more like creepers than anything else. These scarcely hid the surface, which was brown with the remnants of oak-leaves; there seemed so little cover, indeed, that a mouse might have been seen. But at that spot some great spurge-plants hung this way and that, leaning aside, as if the stems were too weak to uphold the heads of dark-green leaves. Thin grasses, perfectly white, bleached by sun and dew, stood in a bunch by the spurge; their seeds had fallen, the last dregs of sap had dried within them, there was nothing left but the bare stalks. A creeper of bramble fenced round one side of the spurge and white grass bunch, and brown leaves were visible on the surface of the ground through the interstices of the spray. It was in the midst of this little thicket that a small, dark, and glittering object caught my attention. I knew it was the eye of some creature at once, but, supposing it nothing more than a young rabbit, was passing on, thinking of other

matters, when it occurred to me, before I could finish
the step I had taken, so quick is thought, that the
eye was not large enough to be that of a rabbit.
I stopped; the black glittering eye had gone—the
creature had lowered its neck, but immediately
noticing that I was looking in that direction, it
cautiously raised itself a little, and I saw at once
that the eye was the eye of a bird. This I knew
first by its size, and next by its position in relation
to the head, which was invisible—for had it been
a rabbit or hare, its ears would have projected.
The moment after, the eye itself confirmed this—
the nictitating membrane was rapidly drawn over
it, and as rapidly removed. This membrane is the
distinguishing mark of a bird's eye. But what bird?
Although I was within two yards, I could not even
see its head, nothing but the glittering eyeball, on
which the light of the sun glinted. The sunbeams
came over my shoulder straight into the bird's face.

Without moving—which I did not wish to do, as it
would disturb the bird—I could not see its plumage;
the bramble spray in front, the spurge behind, and
the bleached grasses at the side, perfectly concealed
it. Only two birds I considered would be likely to
squat and remain quiescent like this—partridge or
pheasant; but I could not contrive to view the least
portion of the neck. A moment afterwards the eye
came up again, and the bird slightly moved its head,
when I saw its beak, and knew it was a pheasant
immediately. I then stepped forward—almost on
the bird—and a young pheasant rose, and flew
between the tree-trunks to a deep dry watercourse,

where it disappeared under some withering yellow ferns.

Of course I could easily have solved the problem long before, merely by startling the bird; but what would have been the pleasure of that? Any plough-lad could have forced the bird to rise, and would have recognized it as a pheasant; to me, the pleasure consisted in discovering it under every difficulty. That was woodcraft; to kick the bird up would have been simply nothing at all. Now I found why I could not see the pheasant's neck or body; it was not really concealed, but shaded out by the mingled hues of white grasses, the brown leaves of the surface, and the general gray-brown tints. Now it was gone, there was a vacant space—its plumage had filled up that vacant space with hues so similar, that, at no farther distance than two yards, I did not recognize it by colour. Had the bird fully carried out its instinct of concealment, and kept its head down as well as its body, I should have passed it. Nor should I have seen its head if it had looked the other way; the eye betrayed its presence. The dark glittering eye, which the sunlight touched, caught my attention instantly. There is nothing like an eye in inanimate nature; no flower, no speck on a bough, no gleaming stone wet with dew, nothing, indeed, to which it can be compared. The eye betrayed it; I could not overlook an eye. Neither nature nor inherited experience had taught the pheasant to hide its eye; the bird not only wished to conceal itself, but to watch my motions, and, looking up from its cover, was immediately observed.

At a turn of the lane there was a great heap of oak
"chumps," crooked logs, sawn in lengths, and piled
together. They were so crooked, it was difficult to
find a seat, till I hit on one larger than the rest.
The pile of "chunks" rose halfway up the stem of
an oak-tree, and formed a wall of wood at my back;
the oak-boughs reached over and made a pleasant
shade. The sun was warm enough to render resting
in the open air delicious, the wind cool enough to
prevent the heat becoming too great; the pile of
timber kept off the draught, so that I could stay and
listen to the gentle "hush, rush" of the breeze in the
oak above me; "hush" as it came slowly, "rush"
as it came fast, and a low undertone as it nearly
ceased. So thick were the haws on a bush of thorn
opposite, that they tinted the hedge a red colour
among the yellowing hawthorn-leaves. To this red
hue the blackberries that were not ripe, the thick dry
red sorrel stalks, a bright canker on a brier almost as
bright as a rose, added their colours. Already the
foliage of the bushes had been thinned, and it was
possible to see through the upper parts of the boughs.
The sunlight, therefore, not only touched their outer
surfaces, but passed through and lit up the branches
within, and the wild-fruit upon them. Though the
sky was clear and blue between the clouds, that is,
without mist or haze, the sunbeams were coloured
the faintest yellow, as they always are on a ripe
autumn day. This yellow shone back from grass
and leaves, from bough and tree-trunk, and seemed
to stain the ground. It is very pleasant to the eyes,
a soft, delicate light, that gives another beauty to the

atmosphere. Some roan cows were wandering down
the lane, feeding on the herbage at the side; their
colour, too, was lit up by the peculiar light, which gave
a singular softness to the large shadows of the trees
upon the sward. In a meadow by the wood the oaks
cast broad shadows on the short velvety sward, not so
sharp and definite as those of summer, but tender,
and, as it were, drawn with a loving hand. They
were large shadows, though it was mid-day—a sign
that the sun was no longer at his greatest height,
but declining. In July, they would scarcely have
extended beyond the rim of the boughs; the rays
would have dropped perpendicularly, now they
slanted. Pleasant as it was, there was regret in the
thought that the summer was going fast. Another
sign—the grass by the gateway, an acre of it, was
brightly yellow with hawkweeds, and under these
were the last faded brown heads of meadow clover;
the brown, the bright yellow disks, the green grass,
the tinted sunlight falling upon it, caused a wavering
colour that fleeted before the glance.

All things brown, and yellow, and red, are brought
out by the autumn sun; the brown furrows freshly
turned where the stubble was yesterday, the brown
bark of trees, the brown fallen leaves, the brown
stalks of plants; the red haws, the red unripe
blackberries, red bryony berries, reddish-yellow
fungi; yellow hawkweed, yellow ragwort, yellow
hazel-leaves, elms, spots in lime or beech; not a
speck of yellow, red, or brown the yellow sunlight
does not find out. And these make autumn, with
the caw of rooks, the peculiar autumn caw of laziness

and full feeding, the sky blue as March between the great masses of dry cloud floating over, the mist in the distant valleys, the tinkle of traces as the plough turns, and the silence of the woodland birds. The lark calls as he rises from the earth, the swallows still wheeling call as they go over, but the woodland birds are mostly still, and the restless sparrows gone forth in a cloud to the stubble. Dry clouds, because they evidently contain no moisture that will fall as rain here; thick mists, condensed haze only, floating on before the wind. The oaks were not yet yellow, their leaves were half green, half brown; Time had begun to invade them, but had not yet indented his full mark.

Of the year there are two most pleasurable seasons : the spring, when the oak-leaves come russet-brown on the great oaks; the autumn, when the oak-leaves begin to turn. At the one, I enjoy the summer that is coming; at the other, the summer that is going. At either, there is a freshness in the atmosphere, a colour everywhere, a depth of blue in the sky, a welcome in the woods. The redwings had not yet come; the acorns were full, but still green; the greedy rooks longed to see them riper. They were very numerous, the oaks covered with them, a crop for the greedy rooks, the greedier pigeons, the pheasants, and the jays.

One thing I missed—the corn. So quickly was the harvest gathered, that those who delight in the colour of the wheat had no time to enjoy it. If any painter had been looking forward to August to enable him to paint the corn, he must have been disappointed.

There was no time; the sun came, saw, and conquered, and the sheaves were swept from the field. Before yet the reapers had entered one field of ripe wheat, I did indeed for a brief evening obtain a glimpse of the richness and still beauty of an English harvest. The sun was down, and in the west a pearly gray light spread widely, with a little scarlet drawn along its lower border. Heavy shadows hung in the foliage of the elms; the clover had closed, and the quiet moths had taken the place of the humming bees. Southwards, the full moon, a red-yellow disk, shone over the wheat, which appeared the finest pale amber. A quiver of colour—an undulation—seemed to stay in the air, left from the heated day; the sunset hues and those of the red-tinted moon fell as it were into the remnant of day, and filled the wheat; they were poured into it, so that it grew in their colours. Still heavier the shadows deepened in the elms; all was silence, save for the sound of the reapers on the other side of the hedge, slash—rustle, slash—rustle, and the drowsy night came down as softly as an eyelid.

While I sat on the log under the oak, every now and then wasps came to the crooked pieces of sawn timber, which had been barked. They did not appear to be biting it—they can easily snip off fragments of the hardest oak,—they merely alighted and examined it, and went on again. Looking at them, I did not notice the lane till something moved, and two young pheasants ran by along the middle of the track and into the cover at the side. The grass at the edge which they pushed through closed behind

them, and feeble as it was—grass only—it shut off
the interior of the cover as firmly as iron bars. The
pheasant is a strong lock upon the woods; like one
of Chubb's patent locks, he closes the woods as firmly
as an iron safe can be shut. Wherever the pheasant
is artificially reared, and a great "head" kept up
for battue-shooting, there the woods are sealed. No
matter if the wanderer approach with the most
harmless of intentions, it is exactly the same as if
he were a species of burglar. The botanist, the
painter, the student of nature, all are met with the
high-barred gate and the threat of law. Of course,
the pheasant-lock can be opened by the silver key;
still, there is the fact, that since pheasants have been
bred on so large a scale, half the beautiful woodlands
of England have been fastened up. Where there is
no artificial rearing there is much more freedom;
those who love the forest can roam at their pleasure,
for it is not the fear of damage that locks the gate,
but the pheasant. In every sense, the so-called sport
of battue-shooting is injurious—injurious to the
sportsman, to the poorer class, to the community.
Every true sportsman should discourage it, and indeed
does. I was talking with a thorough sportsman
recently, who told me, to my delight, that he never
reared birds by hand; yet he had a fair supply, and
could always give a good day's sport, judged as any
reasonable man would judge sport. Nothing must
enter the domains of the hand-reared pheasant; even
the nightingale is not safe. A naturalist has recorded
that in a district he visited, the nightingales were
always shot by the keepers and their eggs smashed,

because the singing of these birds at night disturbed
the repose of the pheasants! They also always
stepped on the eggs of the fern-owl, which are laid
on the ground, and shot the bird if they saw it, for
the same reason, as it makes a jarring sound at dusk.
The fern-owl, or goatsucker, is one of the most harmless of birds—a sort of evening swallow—living on
moths, chafers, and similar night-flying insects.

Continuing my walk, still under the oaks and green
acorns, I wondered why I did not meet any one.
There was a man cutting fern in the wood—a labourer
—and another cutting up thistles in a field; but with
the exception of men actually employed and paid,
I did not meet a single person, though the lane I was
following is close to several well-to-do places. I call
that a well-to-do place where there are hundreds of
large villas inhabited by wealthy people. It is true
that the great majority of persons have to attend to
business, even if they enjoy a good income; still,
making every allowance for such a necessity, it is
singular how few, how very few, seem to appreciate
the quiet beauty of this lovely country. Somehow,
they do not seem to see it—to look over it; there is
no excitement in it, for one thing. They can see a
great deal in Paris, but nothing in an English meadow.
I have often wondered at the rarity of meeting any
one in the fields, and yet—curious anomaly—if you
point out anything, or describe it, the interest ex-
hibited is marked. Every one takes an interest, but
no one goes to see for himself. For instance, since
the natural history collection was removed from the
British Museum to a separate building at South

Kensington, it is stated that the visitors to the Museum have fallen from an average of twenty-five hundred a day to one thousand; the inference is, that out of every twenty-five, fifteen came to see the natural history cases. Indeed, it is difficult to find a person who does not take an interest in some department of natural history, and yet I scarcely ever meet any one in the fields. You may meet many in the autumn far away in places famous for scenery, but almost none in the meadows at home.

I stayed by a large pond to look at the shadows of the trees on the green surface of duckweed. The soft green of the smooth weed received the shadows as if specially prepared to show them to advantage. The more the tree was divided—the more interlaced its branches and less laden with foliage, the more it "came out" on the green surface; each slender twig was reproduced, and sometimes even the leaves. From an oak, and from a lime, leaves had fallen, and remained on the green weed; the flags by the shore were turning brown; a tint of yellow was creeping up the rushes, and the great trunk of a fir shone reddish brown in the sunlight. There was colour even about the still pool, where the weeds grew so thickly that the moorhens could scarcely swim through them.

DOWNS.

A GOOD road is recognized as the groundwork of civilization. So long as there is a firm and artificial track under his feet the traveller may be said to be in contact with city and town, no matter how far they may be distant. A yard or two outside the railway in America the primeval forest or prairie often remains untouched, and much in the same way, though in a less striking degree at first sight, some of our own highways winding through Down districts are bounded by undisturbed soil. Such a road wears for itself a hollow, and the bank at the top is fringed with long rough grass hanging over the crumbling chalk. Broad discs of greater knapweed with stalks like wire, and yellow toad-flax with spotted lip grow among it. Grasping this tough grass as a handle to climb up by, the explorer finds a rising slope of sward, and having walked over the first ridge, shutting off the road behind him, is at once out of civilization. There is no noise. Wherever there are men there is a hum, even in the harvest-field; and in the road below, though lonely, there is sometimes the sharp clatter of hoofs or the grating of wheels on flints. But here the long, long slopes, the endless ridges, the gaps between, hazy and indistinct, are absolutely without noise. In the sunny autumn day the peace of the sky overhead is reflected in the silent earth. Looking out over the steep hills, the first impression is of an immense void like the sea; but there are sounds in detail, the twitter of passing swallows, the restless buzz of bees at the thyme, the rush of the air beaten by a ringdove's wings. These only increase the sense of silent peace, for in themselves they soothe; and how minute the bee beside this hill, and the dove to the breadth of the sky! A white speck of thistledown comes upon a current too light to swing a harebell or be felt by the cheek. The furze-bushes are lined with thistledown, blown there by a breeze now still; it is glossy in the sunbeams, and the yellow hawkweeds cluster beneath. The sweet, clear air, though motionless at this height, cools the rays; but the sun seems to pause and neither to rise higher nor decline. It is the space open to the eye which apparently arrests his movement. There is no noise, and there are no men.

Glance along the slope, up the ridge, across to the next, endeavour to penetrate the hazy gap, but no one is visible. In reality it is not quite so vacant; there may, perhaps, be four or five men between this spot and the gap, which would be a pass if the Downs were high enough. One is not far distant; he is digging flints over the ridge, and, perhaps, at this moment rubbing the earth from a corroded Roman coin which he has found in the pit. Another is thatching, for there are three detached wheat-ricks round a spur of the Down a mile away, where the plain is arable, and there, too, a plough is at work. A shepherd is asleep on his back behind the furze a mile in the other direction. The fifth is a lad trudging with a message; he is in the nut-copse, over the next hill, very happy. By walking a mile the explorer may, perhaps, sight one of these, if they have not moved by then and disappeared in another hollow. And when you have walked the mile—knowing the distance by the time occupied in traversing it—if you look back you will sigh at the hopelessness of getting over the hills. The mile is such a little way, only just along one slope and down into the narrow valley strewn with flints and small boulders. If that is a mile, it must be another up to the white chalk quarry yonder, another to the copse on the ridge; and how far is the hazy horizon where the ridges crowd on and hide each other? Like rowing at sea, you row and row and row, and seem where you started—waves in front and waves behind; so you may walk and walk and walk, and still there is the intrenchment on the summit, at the foot of which, well in sight, you were resting some hours ago.

Rest again by the furze, and some goldfinches come calling shrilly and feasting undisturbed upon the seeds of thistles and other plants. The bird-catcher does not venture so far; he would if there was a rail near; but he is a lazy fellow, fortunately, and likes not the weight of his own nets. When the stubbles are ploughed there will be troops of finches and linnets up here, leaving the hedgerows of the valley almost deserted. Shortly the fieldfares

will come, but not generally till the redwings have
appeared below in the valleys; while the fieldfares
go upon the hills, the green plovers, as autumn
comes on, gather in flocks and go down to the plains.
Hawks regularly beat along the furze, darting on a
finch now and then, and owls pass by at night.
Nightjars, too, are down-land birds, staying in woods
or fern by day, and swooping on the moths which
flutter about the furze in the evening. Crows are too
common, and work on late into the shadows. Sometimes, in getting over the low hedges which divide
the uncultivated sward from the ploughed lands, you
almost step on a crow, and it is difficult to guess
what he can have been about so earnestly, for search
reveals nothing—no dead lamb, hare, or carrion, or
anything else is visible. Rooks, of course, are seen,
and larks, and once or twice in a morning a magpie,
seldom seen in the cultivated and preserved valley.
There are more partridges than rigid game preservers
would deem possible where the overlooking, if done
at all, is done so carelessly. Partridges will never
cease out of the land while there are untouched
downs. Of all southern inland game, they afford
the finest sport; for sport in its genuine sense cannot
be had without labour, and those who would get
partridges on the hills must work for them. Shot
down, coursed, poached, killed before maturity in
the corn, still hares are fairly plentiful, and couch
in the furze and coarse grasses. Rabbits have much
decreased; still there are some. But the larger fir
copses, when they are enclosed, are the resort of all
kinds of birds of prey yet left in the south, and,

perhaps, more rare visitors are found there than anywhere else. Isolated on the open hills, such a copse to birds is like an island in the sea. Only a very few pheasants frequent it, and little effort is made to exterminate the wilder creatures, while they are continually replenished by fresh arrivals. Even ocean birds driven inland by stress of weather seem to prefer the downs to rest on, and feel safer there.

The sward is the original sward, untouched, unploughed, centuries old. It is that which was formed when the woods that covered the hills were cleared, whether by British tribes whose markings are still to be found, by Roman smiths working the ironstone (slag is sometimes discovered), by Saxon settlers, or however it came about in the process of the years. Probably the trees would grow again were it not for sheep and horses, but these preserve the sward. The plough has nibbled at it and gnawed away great slices, but it extends mile after mile; these are mere notches on its breadth. It is as wild as wild can be without deer or savage beasts. The bees like it, and the finches come. It is silent and peaceful like the sky above. By night the stars shine, not only overhead and in a narrow circle round the zenith, but down to the horizon; the walls of the sky are built up of them as well as the roof. The sliding meteors go silently over the gleaming surface; silently the planets rise; silently the earth moves to the unfolding east. Sometimes a lunar rainbow appears; a strange scene at midnight, arching over almost from the zenith down into the dark hollow of the valley. At the first glance it seems white, but presently faint prismatic colours are discerned.

Already as the summer changes into autumn there are orange specks on the beeches in the copses, and the firs will presently be leafless. Then those who live in the farmsteads placed at long intervals begin to prepare for the possibilities of the winter. There must be a good store of fuel and provisions, for it will be difficult to go down to the villages. The ladies had best add as many new volumes as they can to the bookshelf, for they may be practically imprisoned for weeks together. Wind and rain are very different here from what they are where the bulwark of the houses shelters one side of the street, or the thick hedge protects half the road. The fury of the storm is unchecked, and nothing can keep out the raindrops which come with the velocity of shot. If snow falls, as it does frequently, it does not need much to obscure the path; at all times the path is merely a track, and the ruts worn down to the white chalk and the white snow confuse the eyes. Flecks of snow catch against the bunches of grass, against the furze-bushes, and boulders; if there is a ploughed field, against every clod, and the result is bewildering. There is nothing to guide the steps, nothing to give the general direction, and once off the track, unless well accustomed to the district, the traveller may wander in vain. After a few inches have fallen the roads are usually blocked, for all the flakes on miles of hills are swept along and deposited into hollows where the highways run. To be dug out now and then in the winter is a contingency the mail-driver reckons as part of his daily life, and the waggons going to and fro frequently pass between high walls of frozen snow. In these wild places, which can scarcely be said to be populated at all, a snow-storm, however, does not block the King's highways and paralyse traffic as London permits itself to be paralysed under similar circumstances. Men are set to work and cut a way through in a very short time, and no one makes the least difficulty about it. But with the tracks that lead to isolated farmsteads it is different; there is not enough traffic to require the removal of the obstruction, and the drifts occasionally accumulate to twenty feet deep. The ladies are imprisoned, and must be thankful if they have got down a box of new novels.

The dread snow-tempest of 1880–81 swept over these places with tremendous fury, and the most experienced shepherds, whose whole lives had been spent going to and fro on the downs, frequently lost their way. There is a story of a waggoner and his lad going slowly along the road after the thaw, and noticing an odd-looking scarecrow in a field. They went to it, and found it was a man, dead, and still standing as he had stiffened in the snow, the clothes hanging on his withered body, and the eyes gone from the sockets, picked out by the crows. It is only one of many similar accounts, and it is thought between twenty and thirty unfortunate persons perished. Such miserable events are of rare occurrence, but show how open, wild, and succourless the country still remains. In ordinary winters it is only strangers who need be cautious, and strangers seldom appear. Even in summer time, however, a stranger, if he stays till dusk, may easily wander for hours. Once off the highway, all the ridges and slopes seem alike, and there is no end to them.

FOREST.

THE beechnuts are already falling in the forest, and the swine are beginning to search for them while yet the harvest lingers. The nuts are formed by midsummer, and now, the husk opening, the brown angular kernel drops out. Many of the husks fall, too; others remain on the branches till next spring. Under the beeches the ground is strewn with the mast as hard almost to walk on as pebbles. Rude and uncouth as swine are in themselves, somehow they look different under trees. The brown leaves amid which they rout, and the brown-tinted fern behind lend something of their colour and smooth away their ungainliness. Snorting as they work with very eagerness of appetite, they are almost wild, approaching in a measure to their ancestors, the savage boars. Under the trees the imagination plays unchecked, and calls up the past as if yew bow and broad arrow were still in the hunter's hands. So little is changed since then. The deer are here still. Sit down on the root of this oak (thinly covered with moss), and on that very spot it is quite possible a knight fresh home from the Crusades may have rested and feasted his eyes on the lovely green glades

of his own unsurpassed England. The oak was there
then, young and strong; it is here now, ancient, but
sturdy. Rarely do you see an oak fall of itself. It
decays to the last stump; it does not fall. The
sounds are the same—the tap as a ripe acorn drops,
the rustle of a leaf which comes down slowly, the
quick rushes of mice playing in the fern. A movement at one side attracts the glance, and there is a
squirrel darting about. There is another at the very
top of the beech yonder out on the boughs, nibbling
the nuts. A brown spot a long distance down the
glade suddenly moves, and thereby shows itself to
be a rabbit. The bellowing sound that comes now
and then is from the stags, which are preparing to
fight. The swine snort, and the mast and leaves
rustle as they thrust them aside. So little is changed:
these are the same sounds and the same movements,
just as in the olden time.

The soft autumn sunshine, shorn of summer glare,
lights up with colour the fern, the fronds of which
are yellow and brown, the leaves, the gray grass,
and hawthorn sprays already turned. It seems as
if the early morning's mists have the power of tinting
leaf and fern, for so soon as they commence the
green hues begin to disappear. There are swathes
of fern yonder, cut down like grass or corn, the
harvest of the forest. It will be used for litter
and for thatching sheds. The yellow stalks—the
stubble—will turn brown and wither through the
winter, till the strong spring shoot comes up and
the anemones flower. Though the sunbeams reach
the ground here, half the green glade is in shadow,

and for one step that you walk in sunlight ten are
in shade. Thus, partly concealed in full day, the
forest always contains a mystery. The idea that
there may be something in the dim arches held up by
the round columns of the beeches lures the footsteps
onwards. Something must have been lately in the
circle under the oak where the fern and bushes
remain at a distance and wall in a lawn of green.
There is nothing on the grass but the upheld leaves
that have dropped, no mark of any creature, but this
is not decisive; if there are no physical signs, there
is a feeling that the shadow is not vacant. In the
thickets, perhaps—the shadowy thickets with front
of thorn—it has taken refuge and eluded us. Still
onward the shadows lead us in vain but pleasant
chase.

These endless trees are a city to the tree-building
birds. The round knot-holes in the beeches, the
holes in the elms and oaks; they find them all out.
From these issue the immense flocks of starlings
which, when they alight on an isolated elm in winter,
make it suddenly black. From these, too, come
forth the tits, not so welcome to the farmer, as he
considers they reduce his fruit crop; and in these
the gaudy woodpeckers breed. With starlings, wood-
pigeons, and rooks the forest is crowded like a city
in spring, but now in autumn it is comparatively
deserted. The birds are away in the fields, some at
the grain, others watching the plough, and following
it so soon as a furrow is opened. But the stoats are
busy—they have not left, nor the weasels; and so
eager are they that, though they hide in the fern at

first, in a minute or two they come out again, and so get shot.

Like the fields, which can only support a certain proportion of cattle, the forest, wide as it seems, can only maintain a certain number of deer. Carrying the same thought further, it will be obvious that the forest, or England in a natural state, could only support a limited human population. Is this why the inhabitants of countries like France, where they cultivate every rood and try to really keep a man to a rood, do not increase in number? Certainly there is a limit in nature which can only be overcome by artificial aid. After wandering for some time in a forest like this, the impression arises that the fauna is not now large enough to be in thorough keeping with the trees—their age and size and number. The breadth of the arboreal landscape requires a longer list of living creatures, and creatures of greater bulk. The stoat and weasel are lost in bramble and fern, the squirrels in the branches; the fox is concealed, and the badger; the rabbit, too, is small. There are only the deer, and there is a wide gap between them and the hares. Even the few cattle which are permitted to graze are better than nothing; though not wild, yet standing in fern to their shoulders and browsing on the lower branches, they are, at all events, animals for the time in nearly a natural state. By watching them it is apparent how well the original wild cattle agreed with the original scenery of the island. One almost regrets the marten and polecat, though both small creatures, and wishes that the fox would come forth more by day. These acres of bracken and impenetrable thickets need more inhabitants; how well they are fitted for the wild boar! Such thoughts are, of course, only thoughts, and we must be thankful that we have as many wild creatures left as we have.

Looking at the soil as we walk, where it is exposed by the roots of a fallen tree, or where there is an old gravel pit, the question occurs whether forests, managed as they are in old countries, ever really increase the fertility of the earth? That decaying vegetation produces a fine mould cannot be disputed; but it seems here that there is no more decaying vegetation than is required for the support of the trees themselves. The leaves that fall—the million million leaves—blown to and fro, at last disappear, absorbed into the ground. So with quantities of the lesser twigs and branches; but these together do not supply more material to the soil than is annually abstracted by the extensive roots of trees, of bushes, and by the fern. If timber is felled, it is removed, and the bark and boughs with it; the stump, too, is grubbed and split for firewood. If a tree dies it is presently sawn off and cut up for some secondary use or other. The great branches which occasionally fall are some one's perquisite. When the thickets are thinned out, the fagots are carted away, and much of the fern is also removed. How, then, can there be any accumulation of fertilizing material? Rather the reverse; it is, if anything, taken away, and the soil must be less rich now than it was in bygone centuries. Left to itself the process would be the reverse, every tree as it fell slowly enriching the spot where it mouldered, and all the bulk of the timber converted into fertile earth. It was in this way that the American forests laid the foundation of the inexhaustible wheat-lands there. But the modern management of a forest tends in the opposite direction—too much is removed; for if it is wished to improve a soil by the growth of timber, something must be left in it besides the mere roots. The leaves, even, are not all left; they have a value for gardening purposes: though, of course, the few cartloads collected make no appreciable difference.

There is always something going on in the forest; and more men are employed than would be supposed. In the winter the selected elms are thrown and the ash poles cut; in the spring the oak timber comes down and is barked; in the autumn the fern is cut. Splitting up wood goes on nearly all the year round, so that you may always hear the axe. No charcoal-burning is practised, but the mere maintenance of the fences, as, for instance, round the pheasant enclosures, gives much to do. Deer need attention in winter, like cattle; the game has its watchers; and ferreting lasts for months. So that the forest is not altogether useless from the point of view of work. But in so many hundred acres of trees these labourers are lost to sight, and do not in the least detract from its wild appearance. Indeed, the occasional ring of the axe or the smoke rising from the woodman's fire accentuates the fact that it is a forest. The oaks keep a circle round their base and stand at a majestic distance from each other, so that the wind and the sunshine enter, and their precincts are sweet and pleasant. The elms gather together, rubbing their branches in the gale till the bark is worn off and the boughs die; the shadow is deep under them, and moist, favourable to rank grass and coarse mushrooms. Beneath the ashes, after the first frost, the air is full of the bitterness of their blackened leaves, which have all come down at once. By the beeches there is little underwood, and the hollows are filled ankle-deep with their leaves. From the pines comes a fragrant odour, and thus the character of each group dominates the surrounding ground. The shade is too much for many flowers, which prefer the nooks of hedgerows. If there is no scope for the use of "express" rifles, this southern forest really is a forest and not an open hillside. It is a forest of trees, and there are no woodlands so beautiful and enjoyable as these, where it is possible to be lost a while without fear of serious consequences; where you can walk without stepping up to the waist in a decayed tree-trunk, or floundering in a bog; where neither venomous snake nor torturing mosquito causes constant apprehensions and constant irritation. To the eye there is nothing but beauty; to the imagination pleasant pageants of old time; to the ear the soothing cadence of the leaves as the gentle breeze goes over. The beeches rear their Gothic architecture; the oaks are planted firm like castles, unassailable. Quick squirrels climb and dart hither and thither, deer cross the distant glade, and, occasionally, a hawk passes like thought.

The something that may be in the shadow or the thicket, the vain, pleasant chase that beckons us on, still leads the footsteps from tree to tree, till by-and-by a lark sings, and, going to look for it, we find the stubble outside the forest—stubble still bright with the blue and white flowers of gray speedwell. One of the earliest to bloom in the spring, it continues till the plough comes again in autumn. Now looking back from the open stubble on the high wall of trees, the touch of autumn here and there is the more visible—oaks dotted with brown, horse chestnuts yellow, maples orange, and the bushes beneath red with haws.

BEAUTY IN THE COUNTRY.

I.—The Making of Beauty.

It takes a hundred and fifty years to make a beauty—a hundred and fifty years out-of-doors. Open air, hard manual labour or continuous exercise, good food, good clothing, some degree of comfort, all of these, but most especially open air, must play their part for five generations before a beautiful woman can appear. These conditions can only be found in the country, and consequently all beautiful women come from the country. Though the accident of birth may cause their register to be signed in town, they are always of country extraction.

Let us glance back a hundred and fifty years, say to 1735, and suppose a yeoman to have a son about that time. That son would be bred upon the hardest fare, but, though hard, it would be plentiful and of honest sort. The bread would be home-baked, the beef salted at home, the ale home-brewed. He would work all day in the fields with the labourers, but he would have three great advantages over them —in good and plentiful food, in good clothing, and in home comforts. He would ride, and join all the athletic sports of the time. Mere manual labour stiffens the limbs, gymnastic exercises render them supple. Thus he would obtain immense strength from simple hard work, and agility from exercise. Here, then, is a sound constitution, a powerful frame, well knit, hardened — an almost perfect physical existence.

He would marry, if fortunate, at thirty or thirty-five, naturally choosing the most charming of his acquaintances. She would be equally healthy and proportionally as strong, for the ladies of those days were accustomed to work from childhood. By custom soon after marriage she would work harder than before, notwithstanding her husband's fair store of guineas in the iron-bound box. The house, the dairy, the cheese-loft, would keep her arms in training. Even since I recollect, the work done by ladies in country houses was something astonishing, ladies by right of well-to-do parents, by right of education and manners. Really, it seems that there is no work a woman cannot do with the best results for herself, always provided that it does not throw a strain upon the loins. Healthy children sprung from such parents, while continuing the general type, usually tend towards a refinement of the features. Under such natural and healthy conditions, if the mother have a good shape, the daughter is finer; if the father be of good height, the son is taller. These children in their turn go through the same open-air training. In the course of years, the family guineas increasing, home comforts increase, and manners are polished. Another generation sees the cast of countenance smoothed of its original ruggedness,

while preserving its good proportion. The hard
chin becomes rounded and not too prominent, the
cheek-bones sink, the ears are smaller, a softness
spreads itself over the whole face. That which was
only honest now grows tender. Again another generation, and it is a settled axiom that the family are
handsome. The country-side as it gossips agrees
that the family are marked out as good-looking.
Like seeks like, as we know; the handsome inter-
marry with the handsome. Still, the beauty has not
arrived yet, nor is it possible to tell whether she
will appear from the female or male branches. But
in the fifth generation appear she does, with the
original features so moulded and softened by time,
so worked and refined and sweetened, so delicate
and yet so rich in blood, that she seems like a new
creation that has suddenly started into being. No
one has watched and recorded the slow process which
has thus finally resulted. No one could do so,
because it has spread over a century and a half.
If any one will consider, they will agree that the
sentiment at the sight of a perfect beauty is as
much amazement as admiration. It is so astound-
ing, so outside ordinary experience, that it wears the
aspect of magic.

A stationary home preserves the family intact, so
that the influences already described have time to
produce their effect. There is nothing uncommon
in a yeoman's family continuing a hundred and
fifty years in the same homestead. Instances are
known of such occupation extending for over two
hundred years; cases of three hundred years may be

found: now and then one is known to exceed that, and there is said to be one that has not moved for six hundred. Granting the stock in its origin to have been fairly well proportioned, and to have been subject for such a lapse of time to favourable conditions, the rise of beauty becomes intelligible.

Cities labour under every disadvantage. First, families have no stationary home, but constantly move, so that it is rare to find one occupying a house fifty years, and will probably become much rarer in the future. Secondly, the absence of fresh air, and that volatile essence, as it were, of woods, and fields, and hills, which can be felt but not fixed. Thirdly, the sedentary employment. Let a family be never so robust, these must ultimately affect the constitution. If beauty appears it is too often of the unhealthy order; there is no physique, no vigour, no richness of blood. Beauty of the highest order is inseparable from health; it is the outcome of health—centuries of health—and a really beautiful woman is, in proportion, stronger than a man. It is astonishing with what persistence a type of beauty once established in the country will struggle to perpetuate itself against all the drawbacks of town life after the family has removed thither.

When such results are produced under favourable conditions at the yeoman's homestead, no difficulty arises in explaining why loveliness so frequently appears in the houses of landed proprietors. Entailed estates fix the family in one spot, and tend, by intermarriage, to deepen any original physical excellence. Constant out-of-door exercise, riding, hunting, shooting, takes the place of manual labour. All the refinements that money can purchase, travel, education, are here at work. That the culture of the mind can alter the expression of the individual is certain; if continued for many generations, possibly it may leave its mark upon the actual bodily frame. Selection exerts a most powerful influence in these cases. The rich and titled have so wide a range to choose from. Consider these things working through centuries, perhaps in a more or less direct manner, since the Norman Conquest. The fame of some such families for handsome features and well-proportioned frames is widely spread, so much so that a descendant not handsome is hardly regarded by the outside world as legitimate. But even with all these advantages beauty in the fullest sense does not appear regularly. Few indeed are those families that can boast of more than one. It is the best of all boasts; it is almost as if the Immortals had especially favoured their house. Beauty has no period; it comes at intervals, unexpected; it cannot be fixed. No wonder the earth is at its feet.

The fisherman's daughter ere now has reached very high in the scale of beauty. Hardihood is the fisherman's talent by which he wins his living from the sea. Tribal in his ways, his settlements are almost exclusive, and his descent pure. The wind washed by the sea enriches his blood, and of labour he has enough. Here are the same constant factors; the stationary home keeping the family intact, the out-door life, the air, the sea, the sun. Refinement is absent, but these alone are so powerful that now and then beauty appears. The lovely Irish girls, again : their forefathers have dwelt on the mountain-side since the days of Fingal, and all the hardships of their lot cannot destroy the natural tendency to shape and enchanting feature. Without those constant factors beauty cannot be, but yet they will not alone produce it. There must be something in the blood which these influences gradually ripen. If it is not there centuries are in vain ; but if it is there then it needs these conditions. Erratic, meteor-like beauty ! for how many thousand years has man been your slave ! Let me repeat, the sentiment at the sight of a perfect beauty is as much amazement as admiration. It so draws the heart out of itself as to seem like magic.

She walks, and the very earth smiles beneath her feet. Something comes with her that is more than mortal ; witness the yearning welcome that stretches towards her from all. As the sunshine lights up the aspect of things, so her presence sweetens the very flowers like dew. But the yearning welcome is, I think, the most remarkable of the evidence that may be accumulated about it. So deep, so earnest, so forgetful of the rest, the passion of beauty is almost sad in its intense abstraction. It is a passion, this yearning. She walks in the glory of young life ; she is really centuries old.

A hundred and fifty years at the least—more probably twice that—have passed away, while from all enchanted things of earth and air this precious-ness has been drawn. From the south wind that breathed a century and a half ago over the green wheat.

From the perfume of the growing grasses waving over honey-laden clover and laughing veronica, hiding the greenfinches, baffling the bee. From rose-loved hedges, woodbine, and cornflower azure-blue, where yellowing wheat-stalks crowd up under the shadow of green firs. All the devious brooklet's sweetness where the iris stays the sunlight; all the wild woods hold of beauty; all the broad hill's thyme and freedom: thrice a hundred years repeated. A hundred years of cowslips, blue-bells, violets; purple spring and golden autumn; sunshine, shower, and dewy mornings; the night immortal; all the rhythm of Time unrolling. A chronicle unwritten and past all power of writing: who shall preserve a record of the petals that fell from the roses a century ago? The swallows to the housetop three hundred times—think a moment of that. Thence she sprang, and the world yearns towards her beauty as to flowers that are past. The loveliness of seventeen is centuries old. Is this why passion is almost sad?

II.—The Force of Form.

Her shoulders were broad, but not too broad—just enough to accentuate the waist, and to give a pleasant sense of ease and power. She was strong, upright, self-reliant, finished in herself. Her bust was full, but not too prominent—more after nature than the dressmaker. There was something, though, of the corset-maker in her waist, it appeared naturally fine, and had been assisted to be finer. But it was in the hips that the woman was perfect:—fulness without

coarseness; large but not big: in a word, nobly
proportioned. Now imagine a black dress adhering
to this form. From the shoulders to the ankles it
fitted "like a glove." There was not a wrinkle, a
fold, a crease, smooth as if cast in a mould, and yet
so managed that she moved without effort. Every
undulation of her figure as she stepped lightly forward
flowed to the surface. The slight sway of the hip as
the foot was lifted, the upward and *inward* movement
of the limb as the knee was raised, the straightening
as the instep felt her weight, each change as the limb
described the curves of walking was repeated in her
dress. At every change of position she was as gracefully draped as before. All was revealed, yet all
concealed. As she passed there was the sense of a
presence—the presence of perfect form. She was
lifted as she moved above the ground by the curves
of beauty as rapid revolution in a curve suspends the
down-dragging of gravity. A force went by—the force
of animated perfect form.

Merely as an animal, how grand and beautiful is
a perfect woman! Simply as a living, breathing
creature, can anything imaginable come near her?

There is such strength in shape—such force in form.
Without muscular development shape conveys the
impression of the greatest of all strength—that is,
of completeness in itself. The ancient philosophy
regarded a globe as the most perfect of all bodies,
because it was the same—that is, it was perfect and
complete in itself—from whatever point it was con-
templated. Such is woman's form when nature's
intent is fulfilled in beauty, and that beauty gives the
idea of self-contained power.

A full-grown woman is, too, physically stronger than a man. Her physique excels man's. Look at her torso, at the size, the fulness, the rounded firmness, the depth of the chest. There is a nobleness about it. Shoulders, arms, limbs, all reach a breadth of make seldom seen in man. There is more than merely sufficient—there is a luxuriance indicating a surpassing vigour. And this occurs without effort. She needs no long manual labour, no exhaustive gymnastic exercise, nor any special care in food or training. It is difficult not to envy the superb physique and beautiful carriage of some women. They are so strong without effort.

III.—An Arm.

A large white arm, bare, in the sunshine, to the shoulder, carelessly leant against a low red wall, lingers in my memory. There was a house roofed with old gray stone slates in the background, and peaches trained up by the window. The low garden wall of red brick—ancient red brick, not the pale, dusty blocks of these days—was streaked with dry mosses hiding the mortar. Clear and brilliant, the gaudy sun of morning shone down upon her as she stood in the gateway, resting her arm on the red wall, and pressing on the mosses which the heat had dried. Her face I do not remember, only the arm. She had come out from dairy work, which needs bare arms, and stood facing the bold sun. It was very large—some might have called it immense—and yet natural and justly proportioned to the woman, her work, and

her physique. So immense an arm was like a revelation of the vast physical proportions which our race
is capable of attaining under favourable conditions.
Perfectly white—white as the milk in which it was
often plunged—smooth and pleasant in the texture of
the skin, it was entirely removed from coarseness.
The might of its size was chiefly by the shoulder;
the wrist was not large, nor the hand. Colossal,
white, sunlit, bare—among the trees and the meads
around—it was a living embodiment of the limbs we
attribute to the first dwellers on earth.

IV.—Lips.

The mouth is the centre of woman's beauty. To
the lips the glance is attracted the moment she
approaches, and their shape remains in the memory
longest. Curve, colour, and substance are the three
essentials of the lips, but these are nothing without
mobility, the soul of the mouth. If neither sculpture,
nor the palette with its varied resources, can convey
the spell of perfect lips, how can it be done in black
letters of ink only? Nothing is so difficult, nothing
so beautiful. There are lips which have an elongated
curve (of the upper one), ending with a slight curl,
like a ringlet at the end of a tress, like those tiny
wavelets on a level sand which float in before the
tide, or like a frond of fern unrolling. In this curl
there lurks a smile, so that she can scarcely open her
mouth without a laugh, or the look of one. These
upper lips are drawn with parallel lines, the verge
is defined by two lines near together, enclosing the

narrowest space possible, which is ever so faintly less coloured than the substance of the lip. This makes the mouth appear larger than it really is; the bow, too, is more flattened than in the pure Greek lip. It is beautiful, but not perfect, tempting, mischievous, not retiring, and belongs to a woman who is never long alone. To describe it first is natural, because this mouth is itself the face, and the rest of the features are grouped to it. If you think of her you think of her mouth only—the face appears as memory acts, but the mouth is distinct, the remainder uncertain. She laughs and the curl runs upwards, so that you must laugh too, you cannot help it. Had the curl gone downwards, as with habitually melancholy people, you might have withstood her smile. The room is never dull where she is, for there is a distinct character in it—a woman—and not a mere living creature, and it is noticeable that if there are five or six or more present, somehow the conversation centres round her.

There was a lady I knew who had lips like these. Of the kind they were perfect. Though she was barely fourteen she was *the* woman of that circle by the magnetism of her mouth. When we all met together in the evening all that went on in some way or other centred about her. By consent the choice of what game should be played was left to her to decide. She was asked if it was not time for some one to sing, and the very mistress of the household referred to her whether we should have another round or go in to supper. Of course, she always decided as she supposed the hostess wished. At supper, if there

was a delicacy on the table it was invariably offered
to her. The eagerness of the elderly gentlemen, who
presumed on their gray locks and conventional harm-
lessness to press their attentions upon her, showed
who was the most attractive person in the room.
Younger men feel a certain reserve, and do not reveal
their inclinations before a crowd, but the harmless
old gentleman makes no secret of his admiration.
She managed them all, old and young, with unconscious tact, and never left the ranks of the other
ladies as a crude flirt would have done. This tact
and way of modestly holding back when so many
would have pushed her too much to the front retained
for her the good word of her own sex. If a dance
was proposed it was left to her to say yes or no,
and if it was not too late the answer was usually
in the affirmative. So in the morning, should we
make an excursion to some view or pleasant wood,
all eyes rested upon her, and if she thought it fine
enough away we went.

Her features were rather fine, but not especially so;
her complexion a little dusky, eyes gray, and dark
hair; her figure moderately tall, slender but shapely.
She was always dressed well; a certain taste marked
her in everything. Upon introduction no one would
have thought anything of her; they would have said,
"insignificant—plain;" in half an hour, "different
to most girls;" in an hour, "extremely pleasant;"
in a day, "a singularly attractive girl;" and so on,
till her empire was established. It was not the
features—it was the mouth, the curling lips, the
vivacity and life that sparkled in them. There is

wine, deep-coloured, strong, but smooth at the surface. There is champagne with its richness continually rushing to the rim. Her lips flowed with champagne. It requires a clever man indeed to judge of men; now how could so young and inexperienced a creature distinguish the best from so many suitors?

OUT OF DOORS IN FEBRUARY.

THE cawing of the rooks in February shows that the
time is coming when their nests will be re-occupied.
They resort to the trees, and perch above the old
nests to indicate their rights; for in the rookery possession is the law, and not nine-tenths of it only.   In
the slow dull cold of winter even these noisy birds
are quiet, and as the vast flocks pass over, night and
morning, to and from the woods in which they roost,
there is scarcely a sound.   Through the mist their
black wings advance in silence, the jackdaws with
them are chilled into unwonted quiet, and unless you
chance to look up the crowd may go over unnoticed.
But so soon as the waters begin to make a sound in
February, running in the ditches and splashing over
stones, the rooks commence the speeches and conver-
sations which will continue till late into the following
autumn.

The general idea is that they pair in February,
but there are some reasons for thinking that the
rooks, in fact, choose their mates at the end of the
preceding summer.   They are then in large flocks,
and if only casually glanced at appear mixed together
without any order or arrangement.   They move on
the ground and fly in the air so close, one beside

the other, that at the first glance or so you cannot distinguish them apart. Yet if you should be lingering along the by-ways of the fields as the acorns fall, and the leaves come rustling down in the warm sunny autumn afternoons, and keep an observant eye upon the rooks in the trees, or on the fresh-turned furrows, they will be seen to act in couples. On the ground couples alight near each other, on the trees they perch near each other, and in the air fly side by side. Like soldiers each has his comrade. Wedged in the ranks every man looks like his fellow, and there seems no tie between them but a common discipline. Intimate acquaintance with barrack or camp life would show that every one had his friend. There is also the mess, or companionship of half a dozen, a dozen, or more, and something like this exists part of the year in the armies of the rooks. After the nest time is over they flock together, and each family of three or four flies in concert. Later on they apparently choose their own particular friends, that is the young birds do so. All through the winter after, say October, these pairs keep together, though lost in the general mass to the passing spectator. If you alarm them while feeding on the ground in winter, supposing you have not got a gun, they merely rise up to the nearest tree, and it may then be observed that they do this in pairs. One perches on a branch and a second comes to him. When February arrives, and they resort to the nests to look after or seize on the property there, they are in fact already paired, though the almanacs put down St. Valentine's day as the date of courtship.

There is very often a warm interval in February,

sometimes a few days earlier and sometimes later,
but as a rule it happens that a week or so of mild
sunny weather occurs about this time. Released
from the grip of the frost, the streams trickle
forth from the fields and pour into the ditches, so
that while walking along the footpath there is a
murmur all around coming from the rush of water.
The murmur of the poets is indeed louder in February
than in the more pleasant days of summer, for then
the growth of aquatic grasses checks the flow and
stills it, whilst in February, every stone, or flint, or
lump of chalk divides the current and causes a vibration. With this murmur of water, and mild time,
the rooks caw incessantly, and the birds at large
essay to utter their welcome of the sun. The wet
furrows reflect the rays so that the dark earth gleams,
and in the slight mist that stays farther away the
light pauses and fills the vapour with radiance.
Through this luminous mist the larks race after each
other twittering, and as they turn aside, swerving in
their swift flight, their white breasts appear for a
moment. As while standing by a pool the fishes
come into sight, emerging as they swim round from
the shadow of the deeper water, so the larks dart over
the low hedge, and through the mist, and pass before
you, and are gone again. All at once one checks his
pursuit, forgets the immediate object, and rises,
singing as he soars. The notes fall from the air over
the dark wet earth, over the dank grass, and broken
withered fern of the hedges, and listening to them it
seems for a moment spring. There is sunshine in the
song: the lark and the light are one. He gives us a

few minutes of summer in February days. In May he rises before as yet the dawn is come, and the sunrise flows down to us under through his notes. On his breast, high above the earth, the first rays fall as the rim of the sun edges up at the eastward hill. The lark and the light are as one, and wherever he glides over the wet furrows the glint of the sun goes with him. Anon alighting he runs between the lines of the green corn. In hot summer, when the open hillside is burned with bright light, the larks are then singing and soaring. Stepping up the hill laboriously, suddenly a lark starts into the light and pours forth a rain of unwearied notes overhead. With bright light, and sunshine, and sunrise, and blue skies the bird is so associated in the mind, that even to see him in the frosty days of winter, at least assures us that summer will certainly return.

Ought not winter, in allegorical designs, the rather to be represented with such things that might suggest hope than such as convey a cold and grim despair? The withered leaf, the snowflake, the hedging bill that cuts and destroys, why these? Why not rather the dear larks for one? They fly in flocks, and amid the white expanse of snow (in the south) their pleasant twitter or call is heard as they sweep along seeking some grassy spot cleared by the wind. The lark, the bird of the light, is there in the bitter short days. Put the lark then for winter, a sign of hope, a certainty of summer. Put, too, the sheathed bud, for if you search the hedge you will find the buds there, on tree and bush, carefully wrapped around with the case which protects them as a cloak. Put, too, the sharp needles of the green corn; let the wind clear it of snow a little way, and show that under cold clod and colder snow the green thing pushes up, knowing that summer must come. Nothing despairs but man. Set the sharp curve of the white new moon in the sky: she is white in true frost, and yellow a little if it is devising change. Set the new moon as something that symbols an increase. Set the shepherd's crook in a corner as a token that the flocks are already enlarged in number. The shepherd is the symbolic man of the hardest winter time. His work is never more important than then. Those that only roam the fields when they are pleasant in May, see the lambs at play in the meadow, and naturally think of lambs and May flowers. But the lamb was born in the adversity of snow. Or you might set the morning star, for it burns and burns and glitters in the winter dawn, and throws forth beams like those of metal consumed in oxygen. There is nought that I know by comparison with which I might indicate the glory of the morning star, while yet the dark night hides in the hollows. The lamb is born in the fold. The morning star glitters in the sky. The bud is alive in its sheath; the green corn under the snow; the lark twitters as he passes. Now these to me are the allegory of winter.

These mild hours in February check the hold which winter has been gaining, and as it were, tear his claws out of the earth, their prey. If it has not been so bitter previously, when this Gulf stream or current of warmer air enters the expanse it may bring forth a butterfly and tenderly woo the first violet into flower.

But this depends on its having been only moderately cold before, and also upon the stratum, whether it is backward clay, or forward gravel and sand. Spring dates are quite different according to the locality, and when violets may be found in one district, in another there is hardly a woodbine-leaf out. The border line may be traced, and is occasionally so narrow, one may cross over it almost at a step. It would sometimes seem as if even the nut-tree bushes bore larger and finer nuts on the warmer soil, and that they ripened quicker. Any curious in the first of things, whether it be a leaf, or flower, or a bird, should bear this in mind, and not be discouraged because he hears some one else has already discovered or heard something.

A little note taken now at this bare time of the kind of earth may lead to an understanding of the district. It is plain where the plough has turned it, where the rabbits have burrowed and thrown it out, where a tree has been felled by the gales, by the brook where the bank is worn away, or by the sediment at the shallow places. Before the grass and weeds, and corn and flowers have hidden it, the character of the soil is evident at these natural sections without the aid of a spade. Going slowly along the footpath—indeed you cannot go fast in moist February—it is a good time to select the places and map them out where herbs and flowers will most likely come first. All the autumn lies prone on the ground. Dead dark leaves, some washed to their woody frames, short gray stalks, some few decayed hulls of hedge fruit, and among these the mars or stocks of the plants that do not

die away, but lie as it were on the surface waiting.
Here the strong teazle will presently stand high;
here the ground-ivy will dot the mound with bluish-
purple. But it will be necessary to walk slowly
to find the ground-ivy flowers under the cover
of the briers. These bushes will be a likely place
for a blackbird's nest; this thick close hawthorn
for a bullfinch; these bramble thickets with remnants
of old nettle stalks will be frequented by the white-
throat after a while. The hedge is now but a lattice-
work which will before long be hung with green.
Now it can be seen through, and now is the time
to arrange for future discovery. In May everything
will be hidden, and unless the most promising places
are selected beforehand, it will not be easy to search
them out. The broad ditch will be arched over,
the plants rising on the mound will meet the green
boughs drooping, and all the vacancy will be filled.
But having observed the spot in winter you can
almost make certain of success in spring.

It is this previous knowledge which invests those
who are always on the spot, those who work much
in the fields or have the care of woods, with their
apparent prescience. They lead the new comer to
a hedge, or the corner of a copse, or a bend of the
brook, announcing beforehand that they feel assured
something will be found there; and so it is. This,
too, is one reason why a fixed observer usually sees
more than one who rambles a great deal and covers
ten times the space. The fixed observer who hardly
goes a mile from home is like the man who sits still
by the edge of a crowd, and by-and-by his lost

companion returns to him. To walk about in search
of persons in a crowd is well known to be the worst
way of recovering them. Sit still and they will often
come by. In a far more certain manner this is the
case with birds and animals. They all come back.
During a twelvemonth probably every creature would
pass over a given locality : every creature that is not
confined to certain places. The whole army of the
woods and hedges marches across a single farm
in twelve months. A single tree—especially an old
tree—is visited by four-fifths of the birds that ever
perch in the course of that period. Every year, too,
brings something fresh, and adds new visitors to the
list. Even the wild sea birds are found inland, and
some that scarce seem able to fly at all are cast far
ashore by the gales. It is difficult to believe that one
would not see more by extending the journey, but,
in fact, experience proves that the longer a single
locality is studied the more is found in it. But you
should know the places in winter as well as in
tempting summer, when song and shade and colour
attract every one to the field. You should face
the mire and slippery path. Nature yields nothing
to the sybarite. The meadow glows with buttercups
in spring, the hedges are green, the woods lovely ;
but these are not to be enjoyed in their full signifi-
cance unless you have traversed the same places
when bare, and have watched the slow fulfilment
of the flowers.

The moist leaves that remain upon the mounds
do not rustle, and the thrush moves among them
unheard. The sunshine may bring out a rabbit,

feeding along the slope of the mound, following the
paths or runs. He picks his way, he does not like
wet. Though out at night in the dewy grass of
summer, in the rain-soaked grass of winter, and
living all his life in the earth, often damp nearly
to his burrows, no time, and no succession of
generations can make him like wet. He endures
it, but he picks his way round the dead fern and
the decayed leaves. He sits in the bunches of long
grass, but he does not like the drops of rain or dew
on it to touch him. Water lays his fur close, and
mats it, instead of running off and leaving him sleek.
As he hops a little way at a time on the mound he
chooses his route almost as we pick ours in the mud
and pools of February. By the shore of the ditch
there still stand a few dry, dead dock stems, with
some dry reddish-brown seed adhering. Some dry
brown nettle stalks remain; some gray and broken
thistles; some teazles leaning on the bushes. The
power of winter has reached its utmost now, and can
go no farther. These bines which still hang in the
bushes are those of the greater bindweed, and will
be used in a month or so by many birds as con-
veniently curved to fit about their nests. The stem
of wild clematis, grey and bowed, could scarcely
look more dead. Fibres are peeling from it, they
come off at the touch of the fingers. The few brown
feathers that perhaps still adhere where the flowers
once were are stained and discoloured by the beating
of the rain. It is not dead: it will flourish again
ere long. It is the sturdiest of creepers, facing the
ferocious winds of the hills, the tremendous rains

that blow up from the sea, and bitter frost, if only
it can get its roots into soil that suits it. In some
places it takes the place of the hedge proper and
becomes itself the hedge. Many of the trunks of the
elms are swathed in minute green vegetation which
has flourished in the winter, as the clematis will in
the summer. Of all, the brambles bear the wild
works of winter best. Given only a little shelter, in
the corner of the hedges or under trees and copses
they retain green leaves till the buds burst again.
The frosts tint them in autumn with crimson, but
not all turn colour or fall. The brambles are the
bowers of the birds; in these still leafy bowers they
do the courting of the spring, and under the brambles
the earliest arum, and cleaver, or avens, push up.
Round about them the first white nettle flowers, not
long now; latest too, in the autumn. The white
nettle sometimes blooms so soon (always according
to locality), and again so late, that there seems but
a brief interval between, as if it flowered nearly all
the year round. So the berries on the holly if let
alone often stay till summer is in, and new berries
begin` to appear shortly afterwards. The ivy, too,
bears its berries far into the summer. Perhaps if
the country be taken at large there is never a time
when there is not a flower of some kind out, in this
or that warm southern nook. The sun never sets,
nor do the flowers ever die. There is life always,
even in the dry fir-cone that looks so brown and
sapless.

The path crosses the uplands where the lapwings
stand on the parallel ridges of the ploughed field like

a drilled company; if they rise they wheel as one, and in the twilight move across the fields in bands, invisible as they sweep near the ground, but seen against the sky in rising over the trees and the hedges. There is a plantation of fir and ash on the slope, and a narrow waggon-way enters it, and seems to lose itself in the wood. Always approach this spot quietly, for whatever is in the wood is sure at some time or other to come to the open space of the track. Wood-pigeons, pheasants, squirrels, magpies, hares, everything feathered or furred, down to the mole, is sure to seek the open way. Butterflies flutter through the copse by it in summer, just as you or I might use the passage between the trees. Towards the evening the partridges may run through to join their friends before roost-time on the ground. Or you may see a covey there now and then, creeping slowly with humped backs, and at a distance not unlike hedgehogs in their motions. The spot therefore should be approached with care; if it is only a thrush out it is a pleasure to see him at his ease and, as he deems, unobserved. If a bird or animal thinks itself noticed it seldom does much, some will cease singing immediately they are looked at. The day is perceptibly longer already. As the sun goes down, the western sky often takes a lovely green tint in this month, and one stays to look at it, forgetting the dark and miry way homewards. I think the moments when we forget the mire of the world are the most precious. After a while the green corn rises higher out of the rude earth.

Pure colour almost always gives the idea of fire, or

rather it is perhaps as if a light shone through as well as colour itself.   The fresh green blade of corn is like this, so pellucid, so clear and pure in its green as to seem to shine with colour.   It is not brilliant—not a surface gleam or an enamel,—it is stained through. Beside the moist clods the slender flags arise filled with the sweetness of the earth.   Out of the darkness under—that darkness which knows no day save when the ploughshare opens its chinks—they have come to the light.   To the light they have brought a colour which will attract the sunbeams from now till harvest. They fall more pleasantly on the corn, toned, as if they mingled with it.   Seldom do we realize that the world is practically no thicker to us than the print of our footsteps on the path.   Upon that surface we walk and act our comedy of life, and what is beneath is nothing to us.   But it is out from that under-world, from the dead and the unknown, from the cold moist ground, that these green blades have sprung.   Yonder a steam-plough pants up the hill, groaning with its own strength, yet all that strength and might of wheels, and piston, and chains, cannot drag from the earth one single blade like these.   Force cannot make it ; it must grow—an easy word to speak or write, in fact full of potency.   It is this mystery of growth and life, of beauty, and sweetness, and colour, starting forth from the clods that gives the corn its power over me.   Somehow I identify myself with it ; I live again as I see it.   Year by year it is the same, and when I see it I feel that I have once more entered on a new life.   And I think the spring, with its green corn, its violets, and hawthorn-leaves, and increasing

song, grows yearly dearer and more dear to this our
ancient earth.   So many centuries have flown ! Now
it is the manner with all natural things to gather as
it were by smallest particles.   The merest grain of
sand drifts unseen into a crevice, and by-and-by
another; after a while there is a heap; a century and
it is a mound, and then every one observes and
comments on it.   Time itself has gone on like this;
the years have accumulated, first in drifts, then in
heaps, and now a vast mound, to which the mountains
are knolls, rises up and overshadows us.   Time lies
heavy on the world.   The old, old earth is glad to
turn from the cark and care of drifted centuries to the
first sweet blades of green.

There is sunshine to-day after rain, and every lark
is singing.   Across the vale a broad cloud-shadow
descends the hillside, is lost in the hollow, and
presently, without warning, slips over the edge,
coming swiftly along the green tips.   The sunshine
follows—the warmer for its momentary absence.
Far, far down in a grassy coomb stands a solitary
cornrick, conical roofed, casting a lonely shadow—
marked because so solitary, and beyond it on the
rising slope is a brown copse.   The leafless branches
take a brown tint in the sunlight; on the summit
above there is furze; then more hill lines drawn
against the sky.   In the tops of the dark pines at the
corner of the copse, could the glance sustain itself to
see them, there are finches warming themselves in the
sunbeams.   The thick needles shelter them from the
current of air, and the sky is bluer above the pines.
Their hearts are full already of the happy days to

come, when the moss yonder by the beech, and the
lichen on the fir-trunk, and the loose fibrés caught in
the fork of an unbending bough, shall furnish forth a
sufficient mansion for their young. Another broad
cloud-shadow, and another warm embrace of sunlight.
All the serried ranks of the green corn bow at the
word of command as the wind rushes over them.

There is largeness and freedom here. Broad as the
down and free as the wind, the thought can roam
high over the narrow roofs in the vale. Nature has
affixed no bounds to thought. All the palings, and
walls, and crooked fences deep down yonder are
artificial. The fetters and traditions, the routine, the
dull roundabout which deadens the spirit like the cold
moist earth, are the merest nothings. Here it is easy
with the physical eye to look over the highest roof.
The moment the eye of the mind is filled with the
beauty of things natural an equal freedom and width
of view come to it. Step aside from the trodden
footpath of personal experience, throwing away the
petty cynicism born of petty hopes disappointed.
Step out upon the broad down beside the green corn,
and let its freshness become part of life.

The wind passes, and it bends—let the wind, too,
pass over the spirit. From the cloud-shadow it
emerges to the sunshine—let the heart come out from
the shadow of roofs to the open glow of the sky. High
above, the songs of the larks fall as rain—receive it
with open hands. Pure is the colour of the green
flags, the slender-pointed blades—let the thought be
pure as the light that shines through that colour.
Broad are the downs and open the aspect—gather the

breadth and largeness of view. Never can that view be wide enough and large enough, there will always be room to aim higher. As the air of the hills enriches the blood, so let the presence of these beautiful things enrich the inner sense. One memory of the green corn, fresh beneath the sun and wind, will lift up the heart from the clods.

HAUNTS OF THE LAPWING.

I.—WINTER.

COMING like a white wall the rain reaches me, and in
an instant everything is gone from sight that is more
than ten yards distant. The narrow upland road
is beaten to a darker hue, and two runnels of water
rush along at the sides, where, when the chalk-laden
streamlets dry, blue splinters of flint will be exposed
in the channels. For a moment the air seems driven
away by the sudden pressure, and I catch my breath
and stand still with one shoulder forward to receive
the blow. Hiss, the land shudders under the cold
onslaught; hiss, and on the blast goes, and the
sound with it, for the very fury of the rain, after
the first second, drowns its own noise. There is
not a single creature visible, the low and stunted
hedgerows, bare of leaf, could conceal nothing; the
rain passes straight through to the ground. Crooked
and gnarled, the bushes are locked together as if in
no other way could they hold themselves against the
gales. Such little grass as there is on the mounds
is thin and short, and could not hide a mouse.
There is no finch, sparrow, thrush, blackbird. As

the wave of rain passes over and leaves a hollow
between the waters, that which has gone and that
to come, the ploughed lands on either side are seen
to be equally bare. In furrows full of water, a hare
would not sit, nor partridge run; the larks, the
patient larks which endure almost everything, even
they have gone. Furrow on furrow with flints dotted
on their slopes, and chalk lumps, that is all. The
cold earth gives no sweet petal of flower, nor can
any bud of thought or bloom of imagination start
forth in the mind. But step by step, forcing a way
through the rain and over the ridge, I find a small
and stunted copse down in the next hollow. It is
rather a wide hedge than a copse, and stands by the
road in the corner of a field. The boughs are bare;
still they break the storm, and it is a relief to wait
a while there and rest. After a minute or so the eye
gets accustomed to the branches and finds a line of
sight through the narrow end of the copse. Within
twenty yards—just outside the copse—there are a
number of lapwings, dispersed about the furrows.
One runs a few feet forward and picks something
from the ground; another runs in the same manner
to one side; a third rushes in still a third direction.
Their crests, their green-tinted wings, and white
breasts are not disarranged by the torrent. Something in the style of the birds recalls the wagtail,
though they are so much larger. Beyond these
are half a dozen more, and in a straggling line
others extend out into the field. They have found
some slight shelter here from the sweeping of the
rain and wind, and are not obliged to face it as in

the open. Minutely searching every clod they gather their food in imperceptible items from the surface.

Sodden leaves lie in the furrows along the side of the copse; broken and decaying burdocks still uphold their jagged stems, but will be soaked away by degrees; dank grasses droop outwards; the red seed of a dock is all that remains of the berries and fruit, the seeds and grain of autumn. Like the hedge, the copse is vacant. Nothing moves within, watch as carefully as I may. The boughs are blackened by wet and would touch cold. From the grasses to the branches there is nothing any one would like to handle, and I stand apart even from the bush that keeps away the rain. The green plovers are the only things of life that save the earth from utter loneliness. Heavily as the rain may fall, cold as the saturated wind may blow, the plovers remind us of the beauty of shape, colour, and animation. They seem too slender to withstand the blast—they should have gone with the swallows —too delicate for these rude hours; yet they alone face them.

Once more the wave of rain has passed, and yonder the hills appear; these are but uplands. The nearest and highest has a green rampart, visible for a moment against the dark sky, and then again wrapped in a toga of misty cloud. So the chilled Roman drew his toga around him in ancient days as from that spot he looked wistfully southwards and thought of Italy. Wee-ah-wee! Some chance movement has been noticed by the nearest bird, and away they go at once as if with the same wings, sweeping

overhead, then to the right, then to the left, and
then back again, till at last lost in the coming shower.
After they have thus vibrated to and fro long enough,
like a pendulum coming to rest, they will alight in
the open field on the ridge behind. There in drilled
ranks, well closed together, all facing the same way,
they will stand for hours. Let us go also and let
the shower conceal them. Another time my path
leads over the hills.

It is afternoon, which in winter is evening. The
sward of the down is dry under foot, but hard, and
does not lift the instep with the springy feel of
summer. The sky is gone, it is not clouded, it is
swathed in gloom. Upwards the still air thickens,
and there is no arch or vault of heaven. Formless
and vague, it seems some vast shadow descending.
The sun has disappeared, and the light there still
is, is left in the atmosphere enclosed by the gloomy
mist as pools are left by a receding tide. Through
the sand the water slips, and through the mist the
light glides away. Nearer comes the formless
shadow, and the visible earth grows smaller. The
path has faded, and there are no means on the open
downs of knowing whether the direction pursued is
right or wrong, till a boulder (which is a landmark)
is perceived. Thence the way is down the slope,
the last and limit of the hills there. It is a rough
descent, the paths worn by sheep may at any moment
cause a stumble. At the foot is a waggon-track
beside a low hedge, enclosing the first arable field.
The hedge is a guide, but the ruts are deep, and it
still needs slow and careful walking. Wee-ah-

wee! Up from the dusky surface of the arable
field springs a plover, and the notes are immediately
repeated by another. They can just be seen as
darker bodies against the shadow as they fly overhead. Wee-ah-wee! The sound grows fainter as
they fetch a longer circle in the gloom.

There is another winter resort of plovers in the
valley where a barren waste was ploughed some years
ago. A few furze bushes still stand in the hedges
about it, and the corners are full of rushes. Not
all the grubbing of furze and bushes, the deep
ploughing and draining, has succeeded in rendering
the place fertile like the adjacent fields. The
character of a marsh adheres to it still. So long
as there is a crop, the lapwings keep away, but as
soon as the ploughs turn up the ground in autumn
they return. The place lies low, and level with the
waters in the ponds and streamlets. A mist hangs
about it in the evening, and even when there is none,
there is a distinct difference in the atmosphere while
passing it. From their hereditary home the lapwings
cannot be entirely driven away. Out of the mist
comes their plaintive cry; they are hidden, and
their exact locality is not to be discovered. Where
winter rules most ruthlessly, where darkness is
deepest in daylight, there the slender plovers stay
undaunted.

II.—Spring.

A soft sound of water moving among thousands
of grass-blades—to the hearing it is as the sweetness
of spring air to the scent. It is so faint and so

diffused that the exact spot whence it issues cannot
be discerned, yet it is distinct, and my footsteps are
slower as I listen. Yonder, in the corners of the
mead, the atmosphere is full of some ethereal vapour.
The sunshine stays in the air there, as if the green
hedges held the wind from brushing it away. Low
and plaintive come the notes of a lapwing; the same
notes, but tender with love.

On this side, by the hedge, the ground is a little
higher and dry, hung over with the lengthy boughs
of an oak, which give some shade. I always feel
a sense of regret when I see a seedling oak in the
grass. The two green leaves—the little stem so
upright and confident, and, though but a few inches
high, already so completely a tree—are in themselves beautiful. Power, endurance, grandeur are
there; you can grasp all with your hand, and take
a ship between the finger and thumb. Time, that
sweeps away everything, is for a while repelled; the
oak will grow when the time we know is forgotten,
and when felled will be the mainstay and safety
of a generation in a future century. That the plant
should start among the grass, to be severed by the
scythe or crushed by cattle, is very pitiful; I cannot
help wishing that it could be transplanted and protected. Of the countless acorns that drop in autumn
not one in a million is permitted to become a tree—
a vast waste of strength and beauty. From the
bushes by the stile on the left hand, which I have
just passed, follows the long whistle of a nightingale.
His nest is near; he sings night and day. Had I
waited on the stile, in a few minutes, becoming used

to my presence, he would have made the hawthorn vibrate, so powerful is his voice when heard close at hand. There is not another nightingale along this path for at least a mile, though it crosses meadows and runs by hedges to all appearance equally suitable; but nightingales will not pass their limits; they seem to have a marked-out range as strictly defined as the lines of a geological map. They will not go over to the next hedge—hardly into the field on one side of a favourite spot, nor a yard farther along the mound. Opposite the oak is a low fence of serrated green. Just projecting above the edge of a brook, fast-growing flags have thrust up their bayonet-tips. Beneath their stalks are so thick in the shallow places that a pike can scarcely push a way between them. Over the brook stand some high maple trees; to their thick foliage wood-pigeons come. The entrance to a coomb, the widening mouth of a valley, is beyond, with copses on the slopes.

Again the plover's notes; this time in the field immediately behind; repeated, too, in the field on the right hand. One comes over, and as he flies he jerks a wing upwards and partly turns on his side in the air, rolling like a vessel in a swell. He seems to beat the air sideways, as if against a wall, not downwards. This habit makes his course appear so uncertain; he may go there, or yonder, or in a third direction, more undecided than a startled snipe. Is there a little vanity in that wanton flight? Is there a little consciousness of the spring-freshened colours of his plumage, and pride in the dainty touch of his wings on the sweet wind? His love is watching

his wayward course. He prolongs it. He has but
a few yards to fly to reach the well-known feeding-
ground by the brook where the grass is short; perhaps
it has been eaten off by sheep. It is a straight and
easy line as a starling would fly. The plover thinks
nothing of a straight line; he winds first with the
course of the hedge, then rises aslant, uttering his
cry, wheels, and returns; now this way, direct at me,
as if his object was to display his snowy breast;
suddenly rising aslant again, he wheels once more,
and goes right away from his object over above the
field whence he came. Another moment and he
returns; and so to and fro, and round and round,
till with a sidelong, unexpected sweep he alights
by the brook. He stands a minute, then utters his
cry, and runs a yard or so forward. In a little while
a second plover arrives from the field behind. He
too dances a maze in the air before he settles. Soon
a third joins them. They are visible at that spot
because the grass is short, elsewhere they would
be hidden. If one of these rises and flies to and
fro almost instantly another follows, and then it is,
indeed, a dance before they alight. The wheeling,
maze-tracing, devious windings continue till the eye
wearies and rests with pleasure on a passing butterfly. These birds have nests in the meadows adjoining; they meet here as a common feeding-ground.
Presently they will disperse, each returning to his
mate at the nest. Half an hour afterwards they will
meet once more, either here or on the wing.

In this manner they spend their time from dawn

through the flower-growing day till dusk. When the sun arises over the hill into the sky already blue the plovers have been up a long while. All the busy morning they go to and fro—the busy morning, when the wood-pigeons cannot rest in the copses on the coomb-side, but continually fly in and out; when the blackbirds whistle in the oaks, when the bluebells gleam with purplish lustre. At noontide, in the dry heat, it is pleasant to listen to the sound of water moving among the thousand thousand grass-blades of the mead. The flower-growing day lengthens out beyond the sunset, and till the hedges are dim the lapwings do not cease.

Leaving now the shade of the oak, I follow the path into the meadow on the right, stepping by the way over a streamlet, which diffuses its rapid current broadcast over the sward till it collects again and pours into the brook. This next meadow is some-what more raised, and not watered; the grass is high and full of buttercups. Before I have gone twenty yards a lapwing rises out in the field, rushes towards me through the air, and circles round my head, making as if to dash at me, and uttering shrill cries. Immediately another comes from the mead behind the oak; then a third from over the hedge, and all those that have been feeding by the brook, till I am encircled with them. They wheel round, dive, rise aslant, cry, and wheel again, always close over me, till I have walked some distance, when, one by one, they fall off, and, still uttering threats, retire. There is a nest in this

meadow, and, although it is, no doubt, a long way
from the path, my presence even in the field, large
as it is, is resented. The couple who imagine their
possessions threatened are quickly joined by their
friends, and there is no rest till I have left their
treasures far behind.

OUTSIDE LONDON.

I.

THERE was something dark on the grass under an elm in the field by the barn. It rose and fell; and we saw that it was a wing—a single black wing, striking the ground instead of the air; indeed, it seemed to come out of the earth itself, the body of the bird being hidden by the grass. This black wing flapped and flapped, but could not lift itself—a single wing of course could not fly. A rook had dropped out of the elm and was lying helpless at the foot of the tree—it is a favourite tree with rooks; they build in it, and at that moment there were twenty or more perched aloft, cawing and conversing comfortably, without the least thought of their dying comrade. Not one of all the number descended to see what was the matter, nor even fluttered half-way down. This elm is their clubhouse, where they meet every afternoon as the sun gets low to discuss the scandals of the day, before retiring to roost in the avenues and tree-groups of the park adjacent. While we looked, a peacock came round the corner of the barn; he had caught sight of the flapping wing, and approached

with long deliberate steps and outstretched neck.
"Ee-aw! Ee-aw! What's this? What's this?" he
inquired in bird-language. "Ee-aw! Ee-aw! My
friends, see here!" Gravely, and step by step, he came
nearer and nearer, slowly, and not without some fear,
till curiosity had brought him within a yard. In a
moment or two a peahen followed and also stretched
out her neck—the two long necks pointing at the
black flapping wing. A second peacock and peahen
approached, and the four great birds stretched out
their necks towards the dying rook—a "crowner's
quest" upon the unfortunate creature.

If any one had been at hand to sketch it, the
scene would have been very grotesque, and not without a ludicrous sadness. There was the tall elm
tinted with yellow, the black rooks high above flying
in and out, yellow leaves twirling down, the blue
peacocks with their crests, the red barn behind, the
golden sun afar shining low through the trees of the
park, the brown autumn sward, a gray horse, orange
maple bushes. There was the quiet tone of the
coming evening—the early evening of October—such
an evening as the rook had seen many a time from
the tops of the trees. A man dies, and the crowd
goes on passing under the window along the street
without a thought. The rook died, and his friends,
who had that day been with him in the oaks feasting
on acorns, who had been with him in the fresh-turned
furrows, born perhaps in the same nest, utterly for-
got him before he was dead. With a great common
caw—a common shout—they suddenly left the tree in
a bevy and flew towards the park. The peacocks

having brought in their verdict, departed, and the dead bird was left alone.

In falling out of the elm, the rook had alighted partly on his side and partly on his back, so that he could only flutter one wing, the other being held down by his own weight. He had probably died from picking up poisoned grain somewhere, or from a parasite. The weather had been open, and he could not have been starved. At a distance, the rook's plumage appears black; but close at hand it will be found a fine blue-black, glossy, and handsome.

These peacocks are the best "rain-makers" in the place; whenever they cry much, it is sure to rain; and if they persist day after day, the rain is equally continuous. From the wall by the barn, or the elm-branch above their cry resounds like the wail of a gigantic cat, and is audible half a mile or more. In the summer, I found one of them, a peacock in the full brilliance of his colours, on a rail in the hedge under a spreading maple bush. His rich-hued neck, the bright light and shadow, the tall green meadow grass, brought together the finest colours. It is curious that a bird so distinctly foreign, plumed for the Asiatic sun, should fit so well with English meads. His splendid neck immediately pleases, pleases the first time it is seen, and on the fiftieth occasion. I see these every day, and always stop to look at them; the colour excites the sense of beauty in the eye, and the shape satisfies the idea of form. The undulating curve of the neck is at once approved by the intuitive judgment of the mind, and it is a pleasure to the mind to reiterate that judgment frequently. It needs no teaching to see its beauty —the feeling comes of itself.

How different with the turkey-cock which struts round the same barn! A fine big bird he is, no doubt; but there is no intrinsic beauty about him; on the contrary, there is something fantastic in his style and plumage. He has a way of drooping his wings as if they were armour-plates to shield him from a shot. The ornaments upon his head and beak are in the most awkward position. He was put together in a dream, of uneven and odd pieces that live and move, but do not fit. Ponderously gawky, he steps as if the world was his, like a "motley" crowned in sport. He is good eating, but he is not beautiful. After the eye has been accustomed to him for some time—after you have fed him every day and come to take an interest in him—after you have seen a hundred turkey-cocks, then he may become passable, or, if you have the fancier's taste, exquisite. Education is requisite first; you do not fall in love at first sight. The same applies to fancy-pigeons, and indeed many pet animals, as pugs, which come in time to be animated with a soul in some people's eyes. Compare a pug with a greyhound straining at the leash. Instantly he is slipped, he is gone as a wave let loose. His flexible back bends and undulates, arches and unarches, rises and falls as a wave rises and rolls on. His pliant ribs open; his whole frame "gives" and stretches, and closing again in a curve, springs forward. Movement is as easy to him as to the wave, which melting, is re-moulded, and sways onward. The curve of the greyhound is not only the line of beauty, but a line which suggests motion; and it is the idea of motion, I think, which so strongly appeals to the mind.

We are often scornfully treated as a nation by people who write about art, because they say we have no taste; we cannot make art jugs for the mantelpiece, crockery for the bracket, screens for the fire; we cannot even decorate the wall of a room as it should be done. If these are the standards by which a sense of art is to be tried, their scorn is to a certain degree just. But suppose we try another standard. Let us put aside the altogether false opinion that art consists alone in something actually made, or painted, or decorated, in carvings, colourings, touches of brush or chisel. Let us look at our lives. I mean to say that there is no nation so thoroughly and earnestly artistic as the English in their lives, their joys, their thoughts, their hopes. Who loves nature like an Englishman? Do Italians care for their pale skies? I never heard so. We go all over the world in search of beauty—to the keen north, to the cape whence the midnight sun is visible, to the extreme south, to the interior of Africa, gazing at the vast expanse of Tanganyika or the marvellous falls of the Zambesi. We admire the temples and tombs and palaces of India; we speak of the Alhambra of Spain almost in whispers, so deep is our reverent admiration; we visit the Parthenon. There is not a picture or a statue in Europe we have not sought. We climb the mountains for their views and the sense of grandeur they inspire; we roam over the wide ocean to the coral islands of the far Pacific; we go deep into the woods of the West; and we stand dreamily under the Pyramids of the East. What part is there of the English year which has not been sung by the poets? all of whom are full of its loveliness; and our greatest of all, Shakspeare, carries, as it were, armfuls of violets, and scatters roses and golden wheat across his pages, which are simply fields written with human life.

This is art indeed—art in the mind and soul, infinitely deeper, surely, than the construction of crockery, jugs for the mantelpiece, dados, or even of paintings. The lover of nature has the highest art in his soul. So, I think, the bluff English farmer who takes such pride and delight in his dogs and horses, is a much greater man of art than any Frenchman preparing with cynical dexterity of hand some coloured presentment of flashy beauty for the *salon*. The English girl who loves her horse—and English girls *do* love their horses most intensely—is infinitely more artistic in that fact than the cleverest painter on enamel. They who love nature are the real artists; the "artists" are copyists. St. John the naturalist, when exploring the recesses of the Highlands, relates how he frequently came in contact with men living in the rude Highland way—forty years since, no education then—whom at first you would suppose to be morose, unobservant, almost stupid. But when they found out that their visitor would stay for hours gazing in admiration at their glens and mountains, their demeanour changed. Then the truth appeared: they were fonder than he was himself of the beauties of their hills and lakes ; they could see the art *there,* though perhaps they had never seen a picture in their lives, certainly not any blue-and-white crockery. The Frenchman flings his fingers dexterously over the canvas, but he has never had that in his heart which the rude Highlander had.

The path across the arable field was covered with a design of birds' feet. The reversed broad arrow of the fore-claws, and the straight line of the hinder claw, trailed all over it in curving lines. In the dry dust, their feet were marked as clearly as a seal on wax—their trails wound this way and that, and crossed as their quick eyes had led them to turn to find something. For fifty or sixty yards the path was worked with an inextricable design; it was a pity to step on it and blot out the traces of those little feet. Their hearts so happy, their eyes so observant, the earth so bountiful to them with its supply of food, and the late warmth of the autumn sun lighting up their life. They know and feel the different loveliness of the seasons as much as we do. Every one must have noticed their joyous-ness in spring; they are quiet, but so very, very busy in the height of summer; as autumn comes on they obviously delight in the occasional hours of warmth. The marks of their little feet are almost sacred—a joyous life has been there—do not obliterate it. It is so delightful to know that something is happy.

The hawthorn hedge that goes down the slope is more coloured than the hedges in the sheltered plain.

Yonder, a low bush on the brow is a deep crimson; the hedge as it descends varies from brown to yellow, dotted with red haws, and by the gateway has another spot of crimson. The lime trees turn yellow from top to bottom, all the leaves together; the elms by one or two branches at a time. A lime tree thus entirely coloured stands side by side with an elm, their boughs intermingling; the elm is green except a line at the outer extremity of its branches. A red light as of fire plays in the beeches, so deep is their orange tint in which the sunlight is caught. An oak is dotted with buff, while yet the main body of the foliage is untouched. With these tints and sunlight, nature gives us so much more than the tree gives. A tree is nothing but a tree in itself: but with light and shadow, green leaves moving, a bird singing, another moving to and fro—in autumn with colour—the boughs are filled with imagination. There then seems so much more than the mere tree; the timber of the trunk, the mere sticks of the branches, the wooden framework is animated with a life. High above, a lark sings, not for so long as in spring—the October song is shorter—but still he sings. If you love colour, plant maple; maple bushes colour a whole hedge. Upon the bank of a pond, the brown oak-leaves which have fallen are reflected in the still deep water.

It is from the hedges that taste must be learned. A garden abuts on these fields, and being on slightly rising ground, the maple bushes, the brown and yellow and crimson hawthorn, the limes and elms, are all visible from it; yet it is surrounded by stiff, straight iron railings, unconcealed even by the grasses, which are carefully cut down with the docks and nettles, that do their best, three or four times in the summer, to hide the blank iron. Within these iron railings stands a row of *arbor vitæ*, upright, and stiff likewise, and among them a few other evergreens; and that is all the shelter the lawn and flower-beds have from the east wind, blowing for miles over open country, or from the glowing sun of August. This garden belongs to a gentleman who would certainly spare no moderate expense to improve it, and yet there it remains, the blankest, barest, most miserable-looking square of ground the eye can find; the only piece of ground from which the eye turns away; for even the potato-field close by, the common potato-field, had its colour in bright poppies, and there were partridges in it, and at the edges, fine growths of mallow and its mauve flowers. Wild parsley, still green in the shelter of the hazel stoles, is there now on the bank, a thousand times sweeter to the eye than bare iron and cold evergreens. Along that hedge, the white byrony wound itself in the most beautiful manner, completely covering the upper part of the thick brambles, a robe thrown over the bushes; its deep cut leaves, its countless tendrils, its flowers, and presently the berries, giving pleasure every time one passed it. Indeed, you could not pass without stopping to look at it, and wondering if any one ever so skilful, even those sure-handed Florentines Mr. Ruskin thinks so much of, could ever draw that intertangled mass of lines. Nor could you easily draw the leaves and head of the great parsley—commonest

of hedge-plants—the deep indented leaves, and the
shadow by which to express them.   There was work
enough in that short piece of hedge by the potato-field
for a good pencil every day the whole summer.   And
when done, you would not have been satisfied with it,
but only have learned how complex and how thoughtful and far reaching Nature is in the simplest of
things.   But with a straight-edge or ruler, any one
could draw the iron railings in half an hour, and a
surveyor's pupil could make them look as well as
Millais himself.   Stupidity to stupidity, genius to
genius; any hard fist can manage iron railings; a
hedge is a task for the greatest.

   Those, therefore, who really wish their gardens or
grounds, or any place, beautiful, must get that greatest
of geniuses, Nature, to help them, and give their
artist freedom to paint to fancy, for it is Nature's
imagination which delights us—as I tried to explain
about the tree, the imagination, and not the fact of
the timber and sticks.   For those white bryony leaves
and slender spirals and exquisitely defined flowers,
are full of imagination, products of a sunny dream,
and tinted so tastefully, that although they are green,
and all about them is green too, yet the plant is quite
distinct, and in no degree confused or lost in the mass
of leaves under and by it.   It stands out, and yet
without violent contrast.   All these beauties of form
and colour surround the place, and try, as it were, to
march in and take possession, but are shut out by
straight iron railings.   Wonderful it is that education
should make folk tasteless!   Such, certainly, seems
to be the case in a great measure, and not in our

own country only, for those who know Italy tell us
that the fine old gardens there, dating back to the
days of the Medici, are being despoiled of ilex and
made formal and straight. Is all the world to be
Versaillised ?

Scarcely two hundred yards from these cold iron
railings, which even nettles and docks would hide if
they could, and thistles strive to conceal, but are not
permitted, there is an old cottage by the roadside.
The roof is of old tile, once red, now dull from
weather; the walls some tone of yellow; the folk are
poor. Against it there grows a vigorous plant of
jessamine, a still finer rose, a vine covers the lean-to
at one end, and tea-plant the corner of the wall;
beside these, there is a yellow-flowering plant, the
name of which I forget at the moment, also trained to
the walls; and ivy. Altogether, six plants grow up
the walls of the cottage; and over the wicket-gate
there is a rude arch—a framework of tall sticks—
from which droop thick bunches of hops. It is a very
commonplace sort of cottage; nothing artistically
picturesque about it, no effect of gable or timber-work;
it stands by the roadside in the most commonplace
way, and yet it pleases. They have called in Nature,
that great genius, and let the artist have his own
way. In Italy, the art-country, they cut down the
ilex trees, and get the surveyor's pupil with straight-
edge and ruler to put it right and square for them.
Our over-educated and well-to-do people set iron
railings round about their blank pleasure-grounds,
which the potato-field laughs at in bright poppies;
and actually one who has some fine park-grounds has

lifted up on high a mast and weather-vane! a thing
useful on the sea-board at coastguard stations for
signalling, but oh! how repellent and straight and
stupid among clumps of graceful elms!

II.

The dismal pits in a disused brickfield, unsightly
square holes in a waste, are full in the shallow
places of an aquatic grass, Reed Canary Grass, I
think, which at this time of mists stretches forth
sharp-pointed tongues over the stagnant water.
These sharp-pointed leaf-tongues are all on one side
of the stalks, so that the most advanced project
across the surface, as if the water were the canvas,
and the leaves drawn on it. For water seems always
to rise away from you—to slope slightly upwards;
even a pool has that appearance, and therefore
anything standing in it is drawn on it as you might
sketch on this paper. You see the water beyond and
above the top of the plant, and the smooth surface
gives the leaf and stalk a sharp, clear definition.
But the mass of the tall grass crowds together, every
leaf painted yellow by the autumn, a thick cover at
the pit-side. This tall grass always awakes my
fancy, its shape partly, partly its thickness, perhaps;
and yet these feelings are not to be analysed. I like
to look at it; I like to stand or move among it on
the bank of a brook, to feel it touch and rustle
against me. A sense of wildness comes with its
touch, and I feel a little as I might feel if there was
a vast forest round about. As a few strokes from

a loving hand will soothe a weary forehead, so the gentle pressure of the wild grass soothes and strokes away the nervous tension born of civilized life.

I could write a whole history of it; the time when the leaves were fresh and green, and the sedge-birds frequented it; the time when the moorhen's young crept after their mother through its recesses; from the singing of the cuckoo by the river, till now brown and yellow leaves strew the water. They strew, too, the dry brown grass of the land, thick tuffets, and lie even among the rushes, blown hither from the distant trees. The wind works its full will over the exposed waste, and drives through the reed-grass, scattering the stalks aside, and scarce giving them time to spring together again, when the following blast a second time divides them.

A cruder piece of ground, ruder and more dismal in its unsightly holes, could not be found; and yet, because of the reed-grass, it is made as it were full of thought. I wonder the painters, of whom there are so many nowadays, armies of amateurs, do not sometimes take these scraps of earth and render into them the idea which fills a clod with beauty. In one such dismal pit—not here—I remember there grew a great quantity of bulrushes. Another was surrounded with such masses of swamp-foliage that it reminded those who saw it of the creeks in semi-tropical countries. But somehow they do not seem to see these things, but go on the old mill-round of scenery, exhausted many a year since. They do not see them, perhaps, because most of those who have educated themselves in the technique of painting are city-bred, and can never have the *feeling* of the country, however fond they may be of it.

In those fields of which I was writing the other day, I found an artist at work at his easel; and a pleasant nook he had chosen. His brush did its work with a steady and sure stroke that indicated command of his materials. He could delineate whatever he selected with technical skill at all events. He had pitched his easel where two hedges formed an angle, and one of them was full of oak-trees. The hedge was singularly full of "bits"— bryony, tangles of grasses, berries, boughs half-tinted and boughs green, hung as it were with pictures like the wall of a room. Standing as near as I could without disturbing him, I found that the subject of his canvas was none of these. It was that old stale and dull device of a rustic bridge spanning a shallow stream crossing a lane. Some figure stood on the bridge—the old, old trick. He was filling up the hedge of the lane with trees from the hedge, and they were cleverly executed. But why drag them into this fusty scheme, which has appeared in every child's sketch-book for fifty years? Why not have simply painted the beautiful hedge at hand, purely and simply, a hedge hung with pictures for any one to copy? The field in which he had pitched his easel is full of fine trees and good "effects." But no; we must have the ancient and effete old story. This is not all the artist's fault, because he must in many cases paint what he can sell; and if his public will only buy effete old stories, he cannot help it. Still, I think if a painter *did* paint that hedge in its fulness of beauty, just simply as it stands in the mellow autumn light, it would win approval of the best people, and that ultimately, a succession of such work would pay.

The clover was dying down, and the plough would soon be among it—the earth was visible in patches. Out in one of these bare patches there was a young mouse, so chilled by the past night that his dull senses did not appear conscious of my presence. He had crept out on the bare earth evidently to feel the warmth of the sun, almost the last hour he would enjoy. He looked about for food, but found none; his short span of life was drawing to a close; even when at last he saw me, he could only run a few inches under cover of a dead clover-plant. Thousands upon thousands of mice perish like this as the winter draws on, born too late in the year to grow strong enough or clever enough to prepare a store. Other kinds of mice perish like leaves at the first blast of cold air. Though but a mouse, to me it was very wretched to see the chilled creature, so benumbed as to have almost lost its sense of danger. There is something so ghastly in birth that immediately leads to death; a sentient creature born only to wither. The earth offered it no help, nor the declining sun; all things organized seem to depend so much on circumstances. Nothing but pity can be felt for thousands upon thousands of such organisms. But thus, too, many a miserable human being has perished in the great Metropolis, dying, chilled and benumbed, of starvation, and finding the hearts of fellow-creatures as bare and cold as the earth of the clover-field.

In these fields outside London the flowers are peculiarly rich in colour. The common mallow, whose flower is usually a light mauve, has here a deep, almost purple bloom; the bird's-foot lotus is a deep orange. The figwort, which is generally two or three feet high, stands in one ditch fully eight feet, and the stem is more than half an inch square. A fertile soil has doubtless something to do with this colour and vigour. The red admiral butterflies, too, seemed in the summer more brilliant than usual. One very fine one, whose broad wings stretched out like fans, looked simply splendid floating round and round the willows which marked the margin of a dry pool. His blue markings were really blue—blue velvet—his red, and the white stroke shone as if sunbeams were in his wings. I wish there were more of these butterflies; in summer, dry summer, when the flowers seem gone and the grass is not so dear to us, and the leaves are dull with heat, a little colour is so pleasant. To me, colour is a sort of food; every spot of colour is a drop of wine to the spirit. I used to take my folding-stool on those long, heated days, which made the summer of 1884 so conspicuous among summers, down to the shadow of a row of elms by a common cabbage-field. Their shadow was nearly as hot as the open sunshine; the dry leaves did not absorb the heat that entered them, and the dry hedge and dry earth poured heat up as the sun poured it down. Dry, dead leaves—dead with heat, as with frost—strewed the grass, dry, too, and withered at my feet.

But among the cabbages, which were very small,

there grew thousands of poppies, fifty times more
poppies than cabbage, so that the pale green of the
cabbage-leaves was hidden by the scarlet petals
falling wide open to the dry air. There was a broad
band of scarlet colour all along the side of the field,
and it was this which brought me to the shade of
those particular elms. The use of the cabbages was
in this way: they fetched for me all the white
butterflies of the neighbourhood, and they fluttered,
hundreds and hundreds of white butterflies, a
constant stream and flow of them over the broad
band of scarlet. Humble-bees came too; bur-bur-
bur; and the buzz, and the flutter of the white
wings over those fixed red butterflies the poppies,
the flutter and sound and colour pleased me in the
dry heat of the day. Sometimes I set my camp-
stool by a humble-bee's nest. I like to see and hear
them go in and out, so happy, busy, and wild; the
humble-bee is a favourite. That summer their nests
were very plentiful; but although the heat might
have seemed so favourable to them, the flies were
not at all numerous, I mean out-of-doors. Wasps,
on the contrary, flourished to an extraordinary
degree. One willow tree particularly took their
fancy; there was a swarm in the tree for weeks,
attracted by some secretion; the boughs and leaves
were yellow with wasps. But it seemed curious that
flies should not be more numerous than usual; they
are dying now fast enough, except a few of the large
ones, that still find some sugar in the flowers of the
ivy. The finest show of ivy flower is among some
yew trees; the dark ivy has filled the dark yew tree,

and brought out its pale yellow-green flowers in the sombre boughs. Last night, a great fly, the last in the house, buzzed into my candle. I detest flies, but I was sorry for his scorched wings; the fly itself hateful, its wings so beautifully made. I have sometimes picked a feather from the dirt of the road and placed it on the grass. It is contrary to one's feelings to see so beautiful a thing lying in the mud. Towards my window now, as I write, there comes suddenly a shower of yellow leaves, wrested out by main force from the high elms; the blue sky behind them, they droop slowly, borne onward, twirling, fluttering towards me—a cloud of autumn butterflies.

A spring rises on the summit of a green brow that overlooks the meadows for miles. The spot is not really very high, still it is the highest ground in that direction for a long distance, and it seems singular to find water on the top of the hill, a thing common enough, but still sufficiently opposed to general impressions to appear remarkable. In this shallow water, says a faint story—far off, faint, and uncertain, like the murmur of a distant cascade—two ladies and some soldiers lost their lives. The brow is defended by thick bramble-bushes, which bore a fine crop of blackberries that autumn, to the delight of the boys; and these bushes partly conceal the sharpness of the short descent. But once your attention is drawn to it, you see that it has all the appearance of having been artificially sloped, like a rampart, or rather a glacis. The grass is green and the sward soft, being moistened by the spring, except in one spot, where the grass is burnt up under the heat of the summer sun, indicating the existence of foundations beneath.

There is a beautiful view from this spot; but leaving that now, and wandering on among the fields, presently you may find a meadow of peculiar shape, extremely long and narrow, half a mile long, perhaps; and this the folk will tell you was the King's Drive, or ride. Stories there are, too, of subterranean passages — there are always such stories in the neighbourhood of ancient buildings—I remember one, said to be three miles long; it led to an abbey. The lane leads on, bordered with high hawthorn hedges, and occasionally a stout hawthorn tree, hardy and twisted by the strong hands of the passing years; thick now with red haws, and the haunt of the red-wings, whose " chuck-chuck " is heard every minute; but the birds themselves always perch on the outer side of the hedge. They are not far ahead, but they always keep on the safe side, flying on twenty yards or so, but never coming to my side.

The little pond, which in summer was green with weed, is now yellow with the fallen hawthorn-leaves; the pond is choked with them. The lane has been slowly descending; and now, on looking through a gateway, an ancient building stands up on the hill, sharply defined against the sky. It is the banqueting hall of a palace of old times, in which kings and princes once sat at their meat after the chase. This is the centre of those dim stories which float like haze over the meadows around. Many a wild red stag has been carried thither after the hunt, and many a wild boar slain in the glades of the forest.

The acorns are dropping now as they dropped five centuries since, in the days when the wild boars fed so greedily upon them; the oaks are broadly touched with brown; the bramble thickets in which the boars hid, green, but strewn with the leaves that have fallen from the lofty trees. Though meadow, arable, and hop-fields hold now the place of the forest, a goodly remnant remains, for every hedge is full of oak and elm and ash; maple too, and the lesser bushes. At a little distance, so thick are the trees, the whole country appears a wood, and it is easy to see what a forest it must have been centuries ago.

The Prince leaving the grim walls of the Tower of London by the Water-gate, and dropping but a short way down with the tide, could mount his horse on the opposite bank, and reach his palace here, in the midst of the thickest woods and wildest country, in half an hour. Thence every morning setting forth upon the chase, he could pass the day in joyous labours, and the evening in feasting, still within call —almost within sound of horn—of the Tower, if any weighty matter demanded his presence.

In our time, the great city has widened out, and comes at this day down to within three miles of the hunting-palace. There still intervenes a narrow space between the last house of London and the ancient Forest Hall, a space of corn-field and meadow; the last house, for although not nominally London, there is no break of continuity in the bricks and mortar thence to London Bridge. London is within a stone's-throw, as it were, and yet, to this day the forest lingers, and it is country. The very atmosphere is different. That smoky thickness characteristic of the suburbs ceases as you ascend the gradual rise, and leave the outpost of bricks and mortar behind. The air becomes clear and strong, till on the brow by the spring on a windy day it is almost like sea-air. It comes over the trees, over the hills, and is sweet with the touch of grass and leaf. There is no gas, no sulphurous acid in that. As the Edwards and Henries breathed it centuries since, so it can be inhaled now. The sun that shone on the red deer is as bright now as then; the berries are thick on the bushes; there is colour in the leaf. The forest is gone; but the spirit of nature stays, and can be found by those who search for it. Dearly as I love the open air, I cannot regret the mediæval days. I do not wish them back again; I would sooner fight in the foremost ranks of Time. Nor do we need them, for the spirit of nature stays, and will always be here, no matter to how high a pinnacle of thought the human mind may attain; still the sweet air, and the hills, and the sea, and the sun, will always be with us.

ON THE LONDON ROAD.

THE road comes straight from London, which is but a very short distance off, within a walk, yet the village it passes is thoroughly a village, and not suburban, not in the least like Sydenham, or Croydon, or Balham, or Norwood, as perfect a village in every sense as if it stood fifty miles in the country. There is one long street, just as would be found in the far west, with fields at each end. But through this long street, and on and out into the open, is continually pouring the human living undergrowth of that vast forest of life, London. The nondescript inhabitants of the thousand and one nameless streets of the unknown east are great travellers, and come forth into the country by this main desert route. For what end? Why this tramping and ceaseless movement? what do they buy, what do they sell, how do they live? They pass through the village street and out into the country in an endless stream on the shutter on wheels. This is the true London vehicle, the characteristic conveyance, as characteristic as the Russian droshky, the gondola at Venice, or the caique at Stamboul. It is the camel of the London desert routes; routes which run right through civilization, but of which daily paper civilization is ignorant.

People who can pay for a daily paper are so far above it; a daily paper is the mark of the man who is in civilization.

Take an old-fashioned shutter and balance it on the axle of a pair of low wheels, and you have the London camel in principle. To complete it add shafts in front, and at the rear run a low freeboard, as a sailor would say, along the edge, that the cargo may not be shaken off. All the skill of the fashionable brougham-builders in Long Acre could not contrive a vehicle which would meet the requirements of the case so well as this. On the desert routes of Palestine a donkey becomes romantic; in a costermonger's barrow he is only an ass; the donkey himself doesn't see the distinction. He draws a good deal of human nature about in these barrows, and perhaps finds it very much the same in Surrey and Syria. For if any one thinks the familiar barrow is merely a truck for the conveyance of cabbages and carrots, and for the exposure of the same to the choice of housewives in Bermondsey he is mistaken. Far beyond that, it is the symbol, the solid expression, of life itself to the owner, his family, and circle of connections, more so than even the ship to the sailor, as the sailor, no matter how he may love his ship, longs for port, and the joys of the shore, but the barrow folk are always at sea on land. Such care has to be taken of the miserable pony or the shame-faced jackass; he has to be groomed, and fed, and looked to in his shed, and this occupies three or four of the family at least, lads and strapping young girls, night and morning. Besides which, the circle of connections look in to see how he is going on, and to hear the story of the day's adventures, and what is proposed for to-morrow. Perhaps one is invited to join the next excursion, and thinks as much of it as others might do of an invitation for a cruise in the Mediterranean. Any one who watches the succession of barrows driving along through the village out into the fields of Kent can easily see how they bear upon their wheels the fortunes of whole families and of their hangers-on. Sometimes there is a load of pathos, of which the race of the ass has carried a good deal in all ages. More often it is a heavy lump of dull, evil, and exceedingly stupid cunning. The wild evil of the Spanish contrabandistas seems atoned by that wildness; but this dull wickedness has no flush of colour, no poppy on its dirt heaps.

Over one barrow the sailors had fixed up a tent— canvas stretched from corner poles, two fellows sat almost on the shafts outside; they were well. Under the canvas there lay a young fellow white and emaciated, whose face was drawn down with severe suffering of some kind, and his dark eyes, enlarged and accentuated, looked as if touched with belladonna. The family council at home in the close and fetid court had resolved themselves into a medical board and ordered him to the sunny Riviera. The ship having been fitted up for the invalid, away they sailed for the south, out from the ends of the earth of London into the ocean of green fields and trees, thence past many an island village, and so to the shores where the Kentish hops were yellowing fast for the pickers. There, in the vintage days, doubtless he found solace, and possibly recovery. To catch a glimpse of that dark and cavernous eye under the shade of the travelling tent reminded me of the eyes of the wounded in the ambulance-waggons that came pouring into Brussels after Sedan. In the dusk of the lovely September evenings—it was a beautiful September, the lime-leaves were just tinted with orange—the waggons came in a long string, the wounded and maimed lying in them, packed carefully, and rolled round, as it were, with wadding to save them from the jolts of the ruts and stones. It is fifteen years ago, and yet I can still distinctly see the eyes of one soldier looking at me from his berth in the waggon. The glow of intense pain—the glow of long-continued agony—lit them up as coals that smouldering are suddenly fanned. Pain brightens the eyes as much as joy, there is a fire in the brain behind it; it is the flame in the mind you see, and not the eyeball. A thought that might easily be rendered romantic, but consider how these poor fellows appeared afterwards. Bevies of them hopped about Brussels in their red-and-blue uniforms, some on crutches, some with two sticks, some with sleeves pinned to their breasts, looking exactly like a company of dolls a cruel child had mutilated, snapping a foot off here, tearing out a leg here, and battering the face of a third. Little men most of them—the bowl of a German pipe inverted would have covered them all, within which, like bees in a hive, they might hum "Te Deum Bismarckum Laudamus." But the romantic flame in the eye is not always so beautiful to feel as to read about.

Another shutter on wheels went by one day with one little pony in the shafts, and a second harnessed in some way at the side, so as to assist in pulling, but without bearing any share of the load. On this shutter eight men and boys balanced themselves; enough for the Olympian height of a four-in-hand. Eight fellows perched round the edge like shipwrecked mariners, clinging to one plank. They were so balanced as to weigh chiefly on the axle, yet in front of such a mountain of men, such a vast bundle of ragged clothes, the ponies appeared like rats.

On a Sunday morning two fellows came along on their shutter: they overtook a girl who was walking on the pavement, and one of them, more sallow and cheeky than his companion, began to talk to her. "That's a nice nosegay, now—give us a rose. Come and ride—there's plenty of room. Won't speak? Now, you'll tell us if this is the road to London Bridge." She nodded. She was dressed in full satin for Sunday; her class think much of satin. She was leading two children, one in each hand, clean and well-dressed. She walked more lightly than a servant does, and evidently lived at home; she did not go to service. Tossing her head, she looked the other way, for you see the fellow on the shutter was dirty, not "dressed" at all, though it was Sunday, poor folks' ball-day; a dirty, rough fellow, with a short clay pipe in his mouth, a chalky-white face—apparently from low dissipation—a disreputable rascal, a monstrously impudent "chap," a true London mongrel. He "cheeked" her; she tossed her head, and looked the other way. But by-and-by she could not help a sly

glance at him, not an angry glance—a look as much
as to say, "You're a man, anyway, and you've the
good taste to admire me, and the courage to speak to
me; you're dirty, but you're a man. If you were well-
dressed, or if it wasn't Sunday, or if it was dark,
or nobody about, I wouldn't mind; I'd let you
'cheek' me, though I have got satin on." The fellow
"cheeked" her again, told her she had a pretty face,
"cheeked" her right and left. She looked away, but
half smiled; she had to keep up her dignity, she did
not feel it. She would have liked to have joined
company with him. His leer grew leerier—the low,
cunning leer, so peculiar to the London mongrel, that
seems to say, "I am so intensely knowing; I am so
very much all there;" and yet the leerer always
remains in a dirty dress, always smokes the coarsest
tobacco in the nastiest of pipes, and rides on a barrow
to the end of his life. For his leery cunning is so
intensely stupid that, in fact, he is as "green" as
grass: his leer and his foul mouth keep him in the
gutter to his very last day. How much more successful plain, simple straightforwardness would be! The
pony went on a little, but they drew rein and waited
for the girl again; and again he "cheeked" her.
Still, she looked away, but she did not make any
attempt to escape by the side-path, nor show resent-
ment. No; her face began to glow, and once or twice
she answered him, but still she would not quite join
company. If only it had not been Sunday—if it had
been a lonely road, and not so near the village, if she
had not had the two tell-tale children with her—she
would have been very good friends with the dirty,

chalky, ill-favoured, and ill-savoured wretch. At the
parting of the roads each went different ways, but she
could not help looking back.

He was a thorough specimen of the leery London
mongrel. That hideous leer is so repulsive—one
cannot endure it—but it is so common; you see it on
the faces of four-fifths of the ceaseless stream that
runs out from the ends of the earth of London into
the green sea of the country. It disfigures the faces
of the carters who go with the waggons and other
vehicles—not nomads, but men in steady employ; it
defaces—absolutely defaces—the workmen who go
forth with vans, with timber, with carpenters' work,
and the policeman standing at the corners, in London
itself particularly. The London leer hangs on their
faces. The Mosaic account of the Creation is dis-
credited in these days, the last revelation took place
at Beckenham ; the Beckenham revelation is superior
to Mount Sinai, yet the consideration of that leer
might suggest the idea of a fall of man even to an
Amœbist. The horribleness of it is in this way, it
hints—it does more than hint, it conveys the leerer's
decided opinion—that you, whether you may be man
or woman, must necessarily be as coarse as himself.
Especially he wants to impress that view upon every
woman who chances to cross his glance. The fist
of Hercules is needed to dash it out of his face.

RED ROOFS OF LONDON.

TILES and tile roofs have a curious way of tumbling
to pieces in an irregular and eye-pleasing manner.
The roof-tree bends, bows a little under the weight,
curves in, and yet preserves a sharpness at each end.
The Chinese exaggerate this curve of set purpose.
Our English curve is softer, being the product of
time, which always works in true taste. The mystery
of tile-laying is not known to every one; for to all
appearance tiles seem to be put on over a thin bed
of hay or hay-like stuff. Lately they have begun to
use some sort of tarpaulin or a coarse material of
that kind; but the old tiles, I fancy, were comfortably
placed on a shake-down of hay. When one slips
off, little bits of hay stick up; and to these the
sparrows come, removing it bit by bit to line their
nests. If they can find a gap they get in, and a
fresh couple is started in life. By-and-by a chimney
is overthrown during a twist of the wind, and half
a dozen tiles are shattered. Time passes; and at
last the tiler arrives to mend the mischief. His labour
leaves a light red patch on the dark dull red of the
breadth about it. After another while the leaks
along the ridge need plastering: mortar is laid on

to stay the inroad of wet, adding a dull white and forming a rough, uncertain undulation along the general drooping curve. Yellow edgings of straw project under the eaves—the work of the sparrows. A cluster of blue-tinted pigeons gathers about the chimney-side; the smoke that comes out of the stack droops and floats sideways, downwards, as if the chimney enjoyed the smother as a man enjoys his pipe. Shattered here and cracked yonder, some missing, some overlapping in curves, the tiles have an aspect of irregular existence. They are not fixed, like slates, as it were for ever : they have a newness, and then a middle-age, and a time of decay like human beings.

One roof is not much; but it is often a study. Put a thousand roofs, say rather thousands of red-tiled roofs, and overlook them—not at a great altitude, but at a pleasant easy angle—and then you have the groundwork of the first view of London over Bermondsey from the railway. I say groundwork, because the roofs seem the level and surface of the earth, while the glimpses of streets are glimpses of catacombs. A city—as something to look at—depends very much on its roofs. If a city have no character in its roofs it stirs neither heart nor thought. These red-tiled roofs of Bermondsey, stretching away mile upon mile, and brought up at the extremity with thin masts rising above the mist—these red-tiled roofs have a distinctiveness, a character; they are something to think about. Nowhere else is there an entrance to a city like this. The roads by which you approach them give you distant aspects—minarets,

perhaps, in the East, domes in Italy; but, coming
nearer, the highway somehow plunges into houses,
confounding you with façades, and the real place is
hidden. Here from the railway you see at once the
vastness of London. Roof-tree behind roof-tree, ridge
behind ridge, is drawn along in succession, line behind
line till they become as close together as the test-lines
used for microscopes. Under this surface of roofs
what a profundity of life there is! Just as the great
horses in the waggons of London streets convey the
idea of strength, so the endlessness of the view
conveys the idea of a mass of life. Life converges
from every quarter. The iron way has many ruts:
the rails are its ruts; and by each of these a ceaseless stream of men and women pours over the tiled
roofs into London. They come from the populous
suburbs, from far-away towns and quiet villages, and
from over sea.

Glance down as you pass into the excavations, the
streets, beneath the red surface: you catch a glimpse
of men and women hastening to and fro, of vehicles,
of horses struggling with mighty loads, of groups at
the corners, and fragments, as it were, of crowds.
Busy life everywhere: no stillness, no quiet, no
repose. Life crowded and crushed together; life
that has hardly room to live. If the train slackens,
look in at the open windows of the houses level with
the line—they are always open for air, smoke-laden
as it is—and see women and children with scarce
room to move, the bed and the dining-table in the
same apartment. For they dine and sleep and work
and play all at the same time. A man works at

night and sleeps by day : he lies yonder as calmly
as if in a quiet country cottage. The children
have no place to play in but the living-room or
the street. It is not squalor—it is crowded life.
The people are pushed together by the necessities
of existence. These people have no dislike to it at
all : it is right enough to them, and so long as
business is brisk they are happy. The man who lies
sleeping so calmly seems to me to indicate the
immensity of the life around more than all the rest.
He is oblivious of it all ; it does not make him nervous
or wakeful ; he is so used to it, and bred to it, that
it seems to him nothing. When he is awake he
does not see it ; now he sleeps he does not hear it.
It is only in great woods that you cannot see the
trees. He is like a leaf in a forest—he is not
conscious of it. Long hours of work have given him
slumber ; and as he sleeps he seems to express by
contrast the immensity and endlessness of the life
around him.

Sometimes a floating haze, now thicker here, and
now lit up yonder by the sunshine, brings out objects
more distinctly than a clear atmosphere. Away there
tall thin masts stand out, rising straight up above
the red roofs. There is a faint colour on them ; the
yards are dark—being inclined, they do not reflect
the light at an angle to reach us. Half-furled canvas
droops in folds, now swelling a little as the wind
blows, now heavily sinking. One white sail is set
and gleams alone among the dusky folds ; for the
canvas at large is dark with coal-dust, with smoke,
with the grime that settles everywhere where men

labour with bare arms and chests. Still and quiet
as trees the masts rise into the hazy air; who would
think, merely to look at them, of the endless labour
they mean? The labour to load, and the labour to
unload; the labour at sea, and the long hours of
ploughing the waves by night; the labour at the
warehouses; the labour in the fields, the mines, the
mountains; the labour in the factories. Ever and
again the sunshine gleams now on this group of
masts, now on that; for they stand in groups as
trees often grow, a thicket here and a thicket yonder.
Labour to obtain the material, labour to bring it
hither, labour to force it into shape—work without
end. Masts are always dreamy to look at: they
speak a romance of the sea; of unknown lands; of
distant forests aglow with tropical colours and
abounding with strange forms of life. In the hearts
of most of us there is always a desire for something
beyond experience. Hardly any of us but have
thought, Some day I will go on a long voyage; but
the years go by, and still we have not sailed.

A WET NIGHT IN LONDON.

OPAQUE from rain drawn in slant streaks by wind and speed across the pane, the window of the railway carriage lets nothing be seen but stray flashes of red lights—the signals rapidly passed. Wrapped in thick overcoat, collar turned up to his ears, warm gloves on his hands, and a rug across his knees, the traveller may well wonder how those red signals and the points are worked out in the storms of wintry London. Rain blown in gusts through the misty atmosphere, gas and smoke-laden, deepens the darkness; the howl of the blast humming in the telegraph wires, hurtling round the chimney-pots on a level with the line, rushing up from the archways; steam from the engines, roar, and whistle, shrieking brakes, and grinding wheels—how is the traffic worked at night in safety over the inextricable windings of the iron roads into the City?

At London Bridge the door is opened by some one who gets out, and the cold air comes in; there is a rush of people in damp coats, with dripping umbrellas, and time enough to notice the archæologically interesting wooden beams which support the roof of the South-Eastern station. Antique beams they are,

good old Norman oak, such as you may sometimes
find in very old country churches that have not been
restored, such as yet exist in Westminster Hall,
temp. Rufus or Stephen, or so. Genuine old woodwork, worth your while to go and see. Take a
sketch-book and make much of the ties and angles
and bolts; ask Whistler or Macbeth, or some one to
etch them, get the Royal Antiquarian Society to pay
a visit and issue a pamphlet; gaze at them reverently
and earnestly, for they are not easily to be matched
in London. Iron girders and spacious roofs are the
modern fashion; here we have the Middle Ages well-
preserved—slam! the door is banged-to, onwards,
over the invisible river, more red signals and rain,
and finally the terminus. Five hundred well-dressed
and civilized savages, wet, cross, weary, all anxious
to get in—eager for home and dinner; five hundred
stiffened and cramped folk equally eager to get out—
mix on a narrow platform, with a train running off
one side, and a detached engine gliding gently after
it. Push, wriggle, wind in and out, bumps from
portmanteaus, and so at last out into the street.

Now, how are you going to get into an omnibus?
The street is "up," the traffic confined to half a
narrow thoroughfare, the little space available at the
side crowded with newsvendors whose contents bills
are spotted and blotted with wet, crowded, too, with
young girls, bonnetless, with aprons over their heads,
whose object is simply to do nothing—just to stand
in the rain and chaff; the newsvendors yell their
news in your ears, then, finding you don't purchase,
they "Yah!" at you; an aged crone begs you to buy

"lights"; a miserable young crone, with pinched face, offers artificial flowers—oh, Naples! Rush comes the rain, and the gas-lamps are dimmed; whoo-oo comes the wind like a smack; cold drops get in the ears and eyes; clean wristbands are splotched; greasy mud splashed over shining boots; some one knocks the umbrella round, and the blast all but turns it. "Wake up!"—"Now then—stop here all night?"—"Gone to sleep?" They shout, they curse, they put their hands to their mouths trumpet-wise and bellow at each other, these cabbies, vanmen, busmen, all angry at the block in the narrow way. The 'bus-driver, with London stout, and plenty of it, polishing his round cheeks like the brasswork of a locomotive, his neck well wound and buttressed with thick comforter and collar, heedeth not, but goes on his round, now fast, now slow, always stolid and rubicund, the rain running harmlessly from him as if he were oiled. The conductor, perched like the showman's monkey behind, hops and twists, and turns now on one foot and now on the other as if the plate were red-hot; now holds on with one hand, and now dexterously shifts his grasp; now shouts to the crowd and waves his hands towards the pavement, and again looks round the edge of the 'bus forwards and curses somebody vehemently. "Near side up! Look alive! Full inside"—curses, curses, curses; rain, rain, rain, and no one can tell which is most plentiful.

The cab-horse's head comes nearly inside the 'bus, the 'bus-pole threatens to poke the hansom in front; the brougham would be careful, for varnish sake, but is wedged and must take its chance; van-wheels catch omnibus hubs; hurry, scurry, whip, and drive; slip, slide, bump, rattle, jar, jostle, an endless stream clattering on, in, out, and round. On, on—" Stanley, on "—the first and last words of cabby's life; on, on, the one law of existence in a London street—drive on, stumble or stand, drive on —strain sinews, crack, splinter—drive on; what a sight to watch as you wait amid the newsvendors and bonnetless girls for the 'bus that will not come! Is it real? It seems like a dream, those nightmare dreams in which you know that you must run, and do run, and yet cannot lift the legs that are heavy as lead, with the demon behind pursuing, the demon of Drive-on. Move, or cease to be—pass out of Time or be stirring quickly; if you stand you must suffer even here on the pavement, splashed with greasy mud, shoved by coarse ruffianism, however good your intentions—just dare to stand still! Ideas here for moralizing, but I can't preach with the roar and the din and the wet in my ears, and the flickering street lamps flaring. That's the 'bus—no; the tarpaulin hangs down and obscures the inscription; yes. Hi! No heed; how could you be so confiding as to imagine conductor or driver would deign to see a signalling passenger; the game is to drive on.

A gentleman makes a desperate rush and grabs the handrail; his foot slips on the asphalte or wood, which is like oil, he slides, his hat totters; happily he recovers himself and gets in. In the block the 'bus is stayed a moment, and somehow we follow, and are landed—" somehow" advisedly. For how do we get into a 'bus? After the pavement, even this

hard seat would be nearly an easy-chair, were it not
for the damp smell of soaked overcoats, the ceaseless
rumble, and the knockings overhead outside. The
noise is immensely worse than the shaking or the
steamy atmosphere, the noise ground into the ears,
and wearying the mind to a state of drowsy narcotism
—you become chloroformed through the sense of
hearing, a condition of dreary resignation and uncom-
fortable ease. The illuminated shops seem to pass
like an endless window without division of doors;
there are groups of people staring in at them in spite
of the rain; ill-clad, half-starving people for the most
part; the well-dressed hurry onwards; they have
homes. A dull feeling of satisfaction creeps over you
that you are at least in shelter; the rumble is a little
better than the wind and the rain and the puddles.
If the Greek sculptors were to come to life again and
cut us out in bas-relief for another Parthenon, they
would have to represent us shuffling along, heads
down and coat-tails flying, splash-splosh—a nation of
umbrellas.

Under a broad archway, gaily lighted, the broad
and happy way to a theatre, there is a small crowd
waiting, and among them two ladies, with their backs
to the photographs and bills, looking out into the
street. They stand side by side, evidently quite
oblivious and indifferent to the motley folk about
them, chatting and laughing, taking the wet and
windy wretchedness of the night as a joke. They
are both plump and rosy-cheeked, dark eyes gleaming
and red lips parted; both decidedly good-looking,
much too rosy and full-faced, too well fed and

comfortable to take a prize from Burne-Jones, very worldly people in the roast-beef sense. Their faces glow in the bright light—merry sea coal-fire faces; they have never turned their backs on the good things of this life. "Never shut the door on good fortune," as Queen Isabella of Spain says. Wind and rain may howl and splash, but here are two faces they never have touched—rags and battered shoes drift along the pavement—no wet feet or cold necks here. Best of all they glow with good spirits, they laugh, they chat; they are full of enjoyment, clothed thickly with health and happiness, as their shoulders—good wide shoulders—are thickly wrapped in warmest furs. The 'bus goes on, and they are lost to view; if you came back in an hour you would find them still there without doubt—still jolly, chatting, smiling, waiting perhaps for the stage, but anyhow far removed, like the goddesses on Olympus, from the splash and misery of London. Drive on.

The head of a great gray horse in a van drawn up by the pavement, the head and neck stand out and conquer the rain and misty dinginess by sheer force of of beauty, sheer strength of character. He turns his head—his neck forms a fine curve, his face is full of intelligence, in spite of the half dim light and the driving rain, of the thick atmosphere, and the black hollow of the covered van behind, his head and neck stand out, just as in old portraits the face is still bright, though surrounded with crusted varnish. It would be a glory to any man to paint him. Drive on.

How strange the dim, uncertain faces of the crowd,

half-seen, seem in the hurry and rain; faces held downwards and muffled by the darkness—not quite human in their eager and intensely concentrated haste. No one thinks of or notices another—on, on—splash, shove, and scramble; an intense selfishness, so selfish as not to be selfish, if that can be understood, so absorbed as to be past observing that any one lives but themselves. Human beings reduced to mere hurrying machines, worked by wind and rain, and stern necessities of life; driven on; something very hard and unhappy in the thought of this. They seem reduced to the condition of the wooden cabs—the mere vehicles—pulled along by the irresistible horse Circumstance. They shut their eyes mentally, wrap themselves in the overcoat of indifference, and drive on, drive on. It is time to get out at last. The 'bus stops on one side of the street, and you have to cross to the other. Look up and down—lights are rushing each way, but for the moment none are close. The gas-lamps shine in the puddles of thick greasy water, and by their gleam you can guide yourself round them. Cab coming! Surely he will give way a little and not force you into that great puddle; no, he neither sees, nor cares, Drive on, drive on. Quick! the shafts! Step in the puddle and save your life!

THE END.

WILDWOOD HOUSE REDISCOVERIES

All titles in the 'Rediscoveries' series
are paperback, 216 × 135mm.

THE ICKNIELD WAY
Edward Thomas
Introduction by Shirley Toulson

Before Edward Thomas was so tragically killed at
Arras in 1917 he had completed some 30 books of
prose and enough poetry to mark him publicly as one
of the most promising poets of his generation.

His reputation in prose was established by his
brilliant evocation of the English countryside, com-
bining as he did 'the mind of an historian, the
sensibility of a poet, and the curiosity of a naturalist'.
These qualities are exemplified in *The Icknield Way*.

This book is, in many ways, the model for the
modern Wildwood Walking Guides such as *The
Oldest Road: An exploration of the Ridgeway* and
*East Anglia: exploring the ley lines and ancient
tracks*. Indeed, topographically speaking, The Icknield Way itself links the Marlborough Downs with
East Anglia and the book evokes the area as it was
more than half a century ago. Illustrated with
excellent line drawings.

ISBN 0 7045 0407 9   £2.95

THE BOOK OF A NATURALIST
W. H. Hudson
Introduction by David Bellamy

Today's W. H. Hudsons are, one supposes, mostly television natural history presenters and programme makers; people like David Attenborough and David Bellamy. Fifty, sixty, seventy years ago however, natural history writing was 'literary', more discursive and poetic. At its best, late nineteenth-century, early twentieth-century natural history writing exhorted and inspired readers to observe, collect, enjoy and preserve the countryside and its wildlife. And without the like of W. H. Hudson — true scientists and true writers (a rare combination) — such of the English countryside that remains and is protected might have disappeared forever.

These essays live and breathe with as much vitality as when they were first written.

ISBN 0 7045 3044 9   £3.50

CELTIC FOLKLORE
Welsh and Manx
In two Volumes
Sir John Rhys

In an age of radio, television, and the car, of in-
dustrialization and uniformity, cultures and com-
munities no longer have a folklore. The imaginative,
mythic and oral—historic tradition of living cultures
has largely died out.

So, thank goodness for researchers like John Rhys,
eminent philologist and anthropologist, passionate
scholar of Celtic Britain, who in the final decades of
the last century — inspired by early folklorists such as
Campbell, Keightley and Lang — went 'into the field'
to document the then still-living traditions and
traditional beliefs (in fairies, elves and other 'little
people') of the rural Celts of Wales and the Isle of
Mann.

Diligent he was; and these pages are the outcome
of painstaking work — yet never dull, always informed, with a passionate interest and sympathy for
the Celtic peoples, and deeply curious about the
message, meanings and origins of those tales of
underground or underwater kingdoms, fairy realms
adjacent to our own. Rhys is a delightful writer and
we are all in his debt.

Volume I   ISBN 0 7045 0405 7   £5.50
Volume II ISBN 0 7045 0406 5   £4.95

THE BUDDHIST WRITINGS OF
LAFCADIO HEARN
Edited by Kenneth Rexroth

Lafcadio Hearn was an improbable interpreter of East to West, yet one of the most successful and, in his day, one of the most influential. Born in Greece in 1850, he went to Japan in 1890 after a career as a journalist in the U.S.A.

He never returned; instead he married a Japanese woman and became Japanese. His writings reflect his passionate love for the old Japan — the art, traditions and myths; it was this side of Japan he popularized and came to understand.

In his introduction Kenneth Rexroth says of Hearn that, whilst not strictly a *believer*, he did make 'an emotional identification with the Buddhist way of life and with Buddhist cults . . . what he does incomparably is to give his reader a feeling for how Buddhism is *lived* in Japan.'

This selection is a marvellous introduction to the essential Japan; and to the work of an inspiring writer.

ISBN 0 7045 0421 9   £3.95

LIFE AND HABIT
Samuel Butler

As publishers of such notable books as Sir Peter
Medawar's *The Life Science* and Gregory Bateson's
Mind and Nature, Wildwood has an interest in bio-
logical writings and evolutionary thinking, especially
in ideas that challenge orthodoxy and received
opinion.

Butler was precisely such a thinker. Disregarded by
scientists, and especially by those around Darwin, on
the grounds that he was a 'novelist' and a 'satirist',
he critically examined the new orthodoxies of
evolutionism. Butler's ideas (and those of Lamarck)
are still alive and potent today. Modern theories of
'the selfish gene' find an echo in Butler's oft-quoted
remark that the chicken is an egg's way of making
another egg. And Butler's ideas still challenge orthodoxy. But whether Butler ('Darwin's finest critic'
Bateson called him) was right or wrong is not the
whole point, rather it is a chance to read contro-
versial scientific writing at its most lucid, witty and
stimulating.

ISBN 0 7045 0425 1   £3.95

THE ROADMENDER
Michael Fairless

This book is extraordinarily difficult to define, to fit into a category. Let us say that it is the work of a mystical visionary, cast in semi-fictional form. It is a valediction written by a young woman who knows she is dying, and a prose-song celebrating life and the preparation for a life to come 'beyond the white gate'.

The Roadmender was widely read and deeply loved when it appeared before the First World War. Now, as then, we are in a spiritual vacuum, we doubt the meaning or value of life, we face the imminent collapse of order and traditional values: we are all, the whole world, facing the 'white gate' and reflecting, before we pass through it, on the richness and joy of life itself. Perhaps we are all 'roadmenders' at the end of the road.

ISBN 0 7045 0431 6   £3.50

HIGHWAYS AND BYWAYS IN DORSET
Sir Frederick Treves
Introduction by Roland Gant

Sir Frederick Treves was an eminent Victorian surgeon, a writer of travel and medical books, and a Dorset man who never lost his feelings for his home county.

To research *Dorset* Sir Frederick cycled over 2,000 miles; his diligent attention to visual detail and historical accuracy displays a true craftsman at work. Dorset may have changed much since 1914 when Treves published *Highways and Byways*, but writing such as this endures and, despite the depredations of the twentieth century, this book can serve as a better guide for holiday-makers than most available in the high streets of Poole or Wareham.

ISBN 0 7045 0430 8   £4.50